Network Your Way to Success

Graeme, May 2014

Stay focused on energizing and giving back to your network!

Network Your Way to Success

Charles Ruffolo's Guide to the Power of Networking

Charles D.A. Ruffolo, MPA, The NetworKing

with Shirley Agudo

translated by Anne Marie Westra

Colofon

Copyright ©2011: Charles D.A. Ruffolo – The NetworKing
Publisher: The Networking / Leonon Media
Cover Design:Hans van Ommen,
Inside Cover Design: TP4U
Photographs: Imre Csany, Studio CSANY (www.fotoillustratie.nl)
E-realisatie: Cross Media Solutions - Euradius, Alphen aan den Rijn
Foto Jan Vredenburg (www.fotojanvredenburg.nl)
Edwin Smulders (www.edwinsmulders.showbiznews.nl)
Tycho Muller, TychoEye (www.tychoeye.nl)

ISBN 978 90 71501 00 5

TESTIMONIALS

"Ruf is one of the most 'connected' people I have ever met... And I don't mean connected in the technological way! He is the person to go to when you need to meet a person. He either knows the person, or is in contact with someone who does! His true talent is having all the right contacts, and connecting business and people together. So how did he get to this position? By networking, of course. He truly is The NetworKing!"

- Vanessa Siegal, Managing Director
SpiralFX Web Development,
USA/the Netherlands

"This man is absolutely amazing! You talk to him and while he listens you see his brain 'check his files', and by the time you have finished your sentence he comes up with people you should meet. He never forgets a name and face and sure knows how to match people."

- Theo van Bleijswijk, Theokookt,
The Netherlands

" 'Ruf's' empathy, or capacity to put himself into the personality of someone else, enables him to master the Work of sharing without a Net wherein he could fall. He is a networking entrepreneur or venture networker. It's becoming a new discipline called 'Ruffin'... a state of mind."

- Nicolas de Potter, Brussels,
Belgium

"The first time I met Ruf, I thought this guy is crazy, everybody shaking hands, walking around like a bunny with Duracell superpower cells. But after talking to this 'twister', my thoughts were totally twisted around. The way he works with people is the ultimate thing in networking. My network in The Netherlands and Europe is a large network, but I thought, this guy has a bigger one… how can we connect these networks? So I made a decision to sign up for his club as a Corporate Networker. Then I felt the special way of doing business on the 'Ruf-tops'.

- Marc N. C. Leegwater, M-MAC, The Netherlands

"Charles Ruffolo is a driving force. The combination of his clear business focus in networking, personal values and always remembering to 'give something back' make him a man to admire. It's difficult in every person's life to find the right balance between supporting yourself, your family and finding time to make a positive difference in other people's lives. His approach works. God bless him."

- Dennis Cowles, Dutch Connections,
The Netherlands

'Dynamic,' 'prolific,' 'distinguished,' 'articulate,' are some of the words I would use in my 15-year association with Ruf. He is one of the most dignified men I have ever met. His integrity is beyond reproach. Ruf is a professional in every sense of the word. He is a hard-working individual with high self-esteem. His credibility and truthfulness are without a doubt two of his strongest personality traits. He is genuinely a man of his word."

- Conrad Payne, Financial Readiness Program Manager,
U.S. Government

"Even if you're not blessed with an energizing personality as Ruf himself is, his principles will go a long way for you. Those principles – most notably that 'networking' equals 'giving' – have brought me to the other end of the world, and will probably bring me back too."

- Erik van Vulpen, Regional Director South East Asia,
Brand Strategy, Cheil/Samsung, Singapore

"He truly is The NetworKing, and a living example of how sticking to principles can make you successful. He is enthusiastic, motivated, energetic, very resourceful, has a strong sense of values and, apart from all those things, he is just one of the nicest people I have ever met. ... He has the ability to bring people together and get them to move in the same direction. His can-do mentality and willpower are something a lot of people, including myself, can learn from… There's nobody like Ruf, that's for sure!"

- Natalia de Smalen, Marketer,
The Netherlands

"Ruf is best described by me in the following keywords: enthusiasm, result-focused, driven, a life-is-too-short-so-make-the-most-of-it-while-you-can type of attitude. He is intense, has direct business savvy, and knows his stuff."

- Peter Gowdy, Regional Director, McAfee Security,
Sniffer Technologies,
The Netherlands

"He's the absolute extreme of networking - this man has no inhibitions."

- Ellie Wood–van Malestijn, Ellie Wood Languages,
The Netherlands

"In networking, Ruf has helped me bridge a personal barrier of introducing one to total strangers....Through Ruf, I have also become much more involved in the Giving Back Foundation. Here, I have found the direct link and purpose of the business community for those in our society who have been less fortunate...Ruf really is a great individual – vibrant, alive and who seems to know everyone on this planet and is happy and willing to share his network of people."

- Bram Cool, Finalist IT Group,
The Netherlands

"Ruf is successful in selling a product – networking – that everyone has but is not aware of."

- Marja H. Pronk, Healthcare Consultancy,
The Netherlands

"He's got a good concept, and it takes a lot of energy. He makes things easier for all of us."

- Ron Jong, Canon,
The Netherlands

"Networking does work! I know because I have gained clients by attending Ruf's networking events, using the The Network Club website, and following his principle 'to give' first. Ruf is successful because he knows how to connect people and create business. His generosity and enthusiasm

seem limitless and ensure that once you meet him, you will remember him!"

- Stephanie Ward, Firefly Coaching,
The Netherlands

"Ruf and his network mean a lot to my business. I think it's worth it for every person with business on his or her mind to have such a great network."

- Norbert Ligterink, Hilton Sales,
The Netherlands

"Ruf is a solid rock in the rough world of networking."

- Pim Kaper † , Trade Mark Agency Kaper, Spain
(In the period following the initial publication of this book in 2004, we learned with much regret that Pim Kaper had passed away.)

"By really living his own message, Charles Ruffolo speaks from experience. The application of his approach, in my own way, opens new doors and has increased my awareness of the benefits of networking."

- Michel van Zomeren, Wisdom Information Consultants,
The Netherlands

"The combination of Ruf's passion for people and his ability to teach others how to leverage their networks make him a powerful voice to our students and alumni seeking career and business growth."

- Len Even, Director, Webster University,
The Netherlands

"Ruf is hard to miss. He's a happy, outgoing guy who has no problem introducing himself to you or you to others. Networking was made for him."

- Paul G. White, Managing Director, Europe, Ipswitch B.V.,
The Netherlands

"Never have I met a person that is more 'begeistert,' as the Germans say. His enthusiasm is as big as his network, his knowledge of where to go and whom to speak to is as huge as the amount of people he meets for his own good – and the good of others... for isn't that the same?

If Giving is equal to Networking, then Ruf has given me an attitude I'll never ever lose again."

- Hans Labruyere, Seneca Risk & Security, The Netherlands

"I have been networking a long time – we all do – but after a training session with Ruf, I became aware of the fact that I was doing it. Knowing that I was building on my relationships helped me in improving and extending them.

... I like doing something for people in my network better than having to ask them for something. It always comes back."

- Andreas Schuele, IT Project and Interim Manager,
Ictopus Consultancy, The Netherlands

"Whada guy! Full Tilt Energy Mobile! The man's a dynamo!"

- Sharon O'Connor, Foxgloves Europe,
USA/The Netherlands

"Networking is fun, and Charles Ruffolo has found many ways to combine business with pleasure. He is a living example of putting networking principles into practice."

- Luc Pie
ters, Ability Alliance, The Netherlands

"He's the man. If I need something, I just have to call him."

- Ali Alhassany, Student, The Hague, and recipient of the Giving Back Foundation's "Most Progress Made Award" for 2003.

"Ruf has been a breath of fresh air in networking for me, bringing into often grey, stuffy and very male events the human touch. He livens things up with raffles, performances and jokes as the corporate master of ceremonies, giving people and companies a chance to shine. His creativity has been an inspiration to my own PR planning and activities, and he always has a kind word, a kiss and a hello for everyone."

- Renee Schnitzler, Pure Wellness Programs,
The Netherlands

"He's very open; it's just him. He doesn't have a double agenda. He puts people together very quickly, without any harm."

**- Pascal van der Bosch, LogicaCMG,
The Netherlands**

"Ruf is living proof of a man with a passion and love for what he does."

- Dale Gannaway, Business Attraction, USA

"In my opinion, there are several stages for networking:

1. *It's what you know that matters*
   (working stage, no 'net' utilization).

2. *It's who you know that matters*
   (accent is on building your NETworking).

3. *It's what you do with who you know that matters*
   (accent is on working your netWORKing).

4. *It's about treating your net like a king, while you work it, that matters*
   (NetworKing).

Charles uses the whole range approach."

**- Wimen Alfrink, Hier en Nu, Independent People Solutions,
The Netherlands**

"He's incredible."

**- Riemke de Vries, Director, Alpha Omega, and Volunteer,
Giving Back Foundation,
The Netherlands**

"The world needs a wake-up call. Get the bugle out Ruf, and get us out of bed!"

- Frank & Carmel Maguire, Hearth Communication Group, USA

"Please, please do try this at home... or any other place you meet people."

- Aernoud van de Graaff, Consultant, PinkRoccade, The Netherlands

"Ruf is a well-deserved breath of fresh air for the business world. His sincere and mature enthusiasm makes networking an emotional want instead of a rational must. His concrete and, at the same time, simple commitment to make things work is a wonderful inspiration for many."

- Robert Benninga, Author, Belgium

"Ruf is not only my best friend, but also a person who I admire because of who he is and what he does. He knows to personalize business and give people a special feeling because of who they are, and not only because of what they do. He always says: 'It is not important who you know, but who knows YOU!' And I am proud that he knows ME!"

- Martijn de Looze, Area Manager, Trekpleister, A.S. Watson, The Netherlands

Random comments heard at The Network Club events:

- *"There's nobody like him."*
- *"If you can give one day to Ruf, you've made your day."*
- *"He's colorful."*
- *"Overwhelming enthusiasm."*
- *"He's got charisma!"*
- *"He's persistence personified."*
- *"He's the man!"*

DEDICATION

This book is dedicated to my wife, Herma, first and foremost, and to Joe P., Clara E., Papa, Mama, Tony, Mary, Joe, Gerry, Jackie, Bobby, Jeannie, Hawk, Mike, Fern, Barbara, Kathy, Maureen, Eke, Reina, Wendy, Louis e, Anneke, Shirley, Anne Marie and the entire The NetworKing Network.

- Charles D.A. Ruffolo, MPA,
Professional Networker, Trainer,
Speaker, Author and Publisher

The NetworKing®

A TRIBUTE

Charles, you are many things to many people – charismatic, motivated, kind, gentlemanly, goal-oriented, ambitious, persistent, determined, driven, relentless, uninhibited, genuine, honest, sincere, outgoing, direct, funny, fun-loving, entertaining, friendly, people-oriented, organized, dependable, diligent, positive, energetic, dynamic, a multi-tasker, a problem-solver and a networker bar none.

But all of these things pale in comparison to what you've been to me – *a blessing in disguise*. While ghostwriting this book, I've made more contacts on the road with you than I've probably made in my entire, not short-lived, life.

As I often said to you at the end of each day, "It's been wild." And indeed it has.

Your friend and fellow Pittsburgher,

Shirley J.S. Agudo, Pro/**PR**
Writing & Editing with an Edge
www.shirleyagudo.com
www.bicycle-mania.nl
The Netherlands
shirleyagudo@gmail.com

For a man who has proclaimed himself "The NetworKing," it comes as no surprise that Charles Ruffolo's address has been Rijksweg 1 for years, translated as "Kingdom Way 1," in a country officially known as the Kingdom of the Netherlands.

"Pure fate," Ruffolo insists, "considering that I lived there for more than a decade before 'The NetworKing' became my trademark and my creed."

Somehow, one gets the impression that nothing with this self-made man depends on fate – not if he can help it.

MY NETWORK STORY

How did my participation in Charles Ruffolo's Keynote Session during a business conference lead to a close cooperation as business associates and the translation of his book *Network Your Way To Success*? It's a 'pinch me in the arm' feeling, and I feel much honored to be able to tell my story in this book.

That one particular day – a business conference in Rotterdam, where I had recently started as an entrepreneur – enabled me to gain a lot of knowledge and to become inspired. I had high expectations and, therefore, I was willing to make the two-hour trip from Enschede, also in The Netherlands. And it turned out to be completely true. The inspiring speakers proved to be the cream of the crop, but the one that most impressed me was Charles Ruffolo, 'professional networker, trainer, international speaker, author and publisher', as the announcement stated. As a final Keynote Speaker, this man, who brought former President Clinton several times to The Netherlands, would end the day with an inspiring session about networking.

Although very unusual to me and most of the people there, but when you think about it, quite natural, this American networking guru, known as The NetworKing, who had been living in The Netherlands for over 25 years, personally shook hands with everyone at the entrance. Wow, that was very promising! Dutch and sober-minded, I became enthralled with this 'American show'. What a passionate speaker!

Bravely, I raised my hand when he asked who had come to Rotterdam to make money. And so I became one of his 'victims' who was asked to come forward and have the opportunity to introduce herself to the public, because, according to Charles Ruffolo, "It's not about who you know, but who knows YOU!" Apparently I did it in a way that was reason enough for him to call me "my friend" at the exit, where he was ready again to shake hands with everyone. At that point I knew that I wanted to have the book that had been written by this special man, and about which he had told us – a book entitled Network Your Way To Success.

A few days later, I decided to send him an email and put my new-found knowledge into practice. I had been paying attention when he talked about the skills of 'how to stay in people's minds'. Therefore, my email to the networking master himself was actually full of his own words. I remember very well that I ended with the sentence: "*And if you think I am only writing to you to say thanks, you are wrong. I am writing to you to **do business!***"

– words that he had proclaimed himself. Then I referred him to my own services "doing business". yes 'Ruf' (as he is commonly known) and I have now done that. Thanks to both of us having a military background, the click was there immediately, and from that moment on it all went into rapid-fire change, with subsequent participation in the Network Club Winter Event at the Hilton Hotel in Amsterdam serving as the beginning of a great partnership.

Since that day we met in Rotterdam, I have been organizing Charles Ruffolo's networking training program in my hometown of Enschede; I am translating for The Networking Academy and The Network Club; and I was asked to translate into Dutch this wonderful book about networking that you are now reading. And when I look into the future, I am very excited about the great and wonderful things that have yet to happen, which will further strengthen our partnership. Ruf does not believe in being 'lucky' or 'in the right place at the right time'. On the contrary, he contends that people to whom good things happen usually have set themselves up to succeed. And I can only agree!

Dear Ruf, I want to thank you enormously for all the opportunities you have given me and continue to give. Thanks to you, I can take my business where I've always wanted: seriously practicing my profession and developing myself with optimal mobility, while making money, because "this is business", like you always say. I love working with you; you're my teacher, a 'boss in a million' (although you really think I'm the boss), an extremely honest person – trustworthy and sincere – and very funny. Therefore, I enjoy our great partnership every day.

Ruf, I look forward to the future with great pleasure!

Anne Marie Westra
EPLÚ Management Support,
Professionalism in management support
annemariewestra@e-plu.nl, www.e-plu.nl

TABLE OF CONTENTS

FOREWORD

Charles "Ruf" Ruffolo is a man on the move. He makes things happen. Somehow he got a double dose of energy and enthusiasm at birth – and manages to share this spirit with all those around him.

Toward the end of a successful 20-year military career, he began to think about what he would do next. He joined the American Chamber of Commerce in the Netherlands, and discovered he had a talent for meeting people. He began to build his own network – and then to think consciously about how to do it. He was asked to give speeches on the subject of networking. Eventually, he decided to make networking his business.

Ruf points out that, while we are all born with networks (think family!), we are not born with the ability to energize our networks. He learned how to build and energize his network, and says you can learn as well. This is why he wrote this book – to share what he has learned.

Ruf lives by what he preaches: he says networking is a give and receive process, and he gives back. Inspired by Colin Powell's America's Promise, he founded the Giving Back Foundation, which provides a sense of direction to talented, ethnic minority/immigrant youth. In doing so, he has widened the horizons of these students, showing them what they can be. And of course, he prevailed upon his network to help Giving Back, which we gladly do!

Buford Alexander
Amsterdam, December 2003

Buford Alexander is a past president of the American Chamber of Commerce in the Netherlands and has served on the Giving Back board of directors. He is a Management Consultant based in Amsterdam.

INTRODUCTION

Whether or not you realize it, you already network. Everyone does. It's a birthright, a given, the silver spoon you may not know thought you have.

The question is: Do you know how to maximize your network to benefit both you and your lifelong circle of connections?

Network Your Way to Success will show you how to network in every facet of your life. It will help you to achieve all of your goals while enabling you to give back in a multitude of ways.

No matter what your age, your status or your particular desires, you can make networking an integral part of your everyday life – a life that will never be the same thereafter.

Go on …put that silver spoon in your mouth. It's been yours all along. Partake.

"People often suggest that networking is an American way of doing business, because Americans easily make contact, but I don't believe in stereotyping this way, because then you're convincing yourself that you can't do it if you're not 'American'. ANYBODY CAN NETWORK ... I provide the platform."

Charles D.A. Ruffolo, MPA
Quoted from *XPat Journal*, September 2001
Van Essen Publishing Concepts and Services
The Hague, Netherlands

CHAPTER 1:

WHAT IS NETWORKING AND WHY DO IT?

"Networking is by far the easiest, most efficient and least expensive way to success ... no matter what your goal."

- Charles Ruffolo, The NetworKing

Where did you go yesterday and to whom did you talk? Did you make any new connections? If not, why? Too shy? Just don't know how to connect? Don't think it's that important?

Maybe your response is that you honestly don't have the time or you simply can't be bothered --- *or*, worse yet, you're convinced that networking is just not for you.

Wake-up call

Whether you realize it or not, you're missing out on a whole dimension of life. As a Professional Networker, Trainer, Speaker, Author and Publisher, I can guarantee that *every single person with whom you come in contact has some connection to your life*. Networking helps you discover that connection. If you remain isolated in your own vacuum and don't intentionally reach out to people by networking, your life will be stripped of the infinite opportunities inherently available through a multitude of daily interactions.

Throughout each and every day, there are countless opportunities to connect you to people, places and things that can benefit your life and, in turn, benefit others. Will you choose to ignore those opportunities or will you choose to *network your way to success*?

Anyone can network... and everyone does!

Good news is that anyone can network and, in fact, you already do. Networking is the silver spoon that you were born with and, regardless of your nationality, status, career, inclination, wealth or lack of it, that spoon can feed you in greater ways than you've ever imagined. Once you become aware of the choices served up by a menu of effective networking, you'll never go back to a diet without it.

Unfortunately, the power of your everyday connections often goes totally unrecognized and untapped. If fostered, these connections,can change your life if you acknowledge their power and utilize them properly. The alternative is to live with broken threads.

Fortunately, networking works for children, college students, housewives and househusbands, the successful and those who aspire to success, the maid and the master, the idolized and the indigent. It is by no means limited to the corporate executive or the already influential person. In fact, that's precisely my aim in writing this book – to show the average person how to network just as easily and effectively as the person who seems to have all the right bells and whistles already at his or her disposal. There is absolutely no one – I repeat, *no one*, exempt from the pervasive power of networking.

Once you learn the simple but practical art of networking set forth in this guide, you'll never regard casual interactions in the same way again. Once you get into the habit of networking, you'll realize that anything – and everything – is possible.

What *is* networking?

Webster defines networking as "making connections among people or groups of a like kind." I say that networking is being able to help or benefit from contacts with individuals with whom you have a direct or indirect relationship, in short, a positive process of mutual support. It's about linking common interests that surface throughout life, about making connections among people you meet on a daily basis. It's about gathering and exchanging information, assistance, ideas, resources and advice. It's about benefiting from those vital links, and giving back in return.

Networking is not rocket science. It's a common sense way of life. But you have to learn the ropes or the loop of success won't swing your way.

Networking is, indeed, a behavioral and organizational skill, but those are just fancy terms for something so basic and commonplace that you already do it without thinking. The problem is that you most likely network on such a nominal basis that you may not recognize it and, therefore, it barely impacts your life the way it could.

Networking is a philosophy of life. It's about not settling for the status quo. It's a philosophy built on trust, respect, honesty, integrity and making things happen with a lot of enthusiasm. It's an art of interacting with and influencing people while listening to their needs and wishes. And it's a science of chemistry between people in all walks of life. It's pure and practical and, above all, it works.

Contrary to popular opinion, networking is a lot more than marketing or selling. It's literally a way of life. Personally, networking helps me to deal with some of life's minor annoyances as well as with my most challenging obstacles and opportunities. It helps me to identify clients and increase my profitability. It means exposure for me – as it will for you – in untold ways.

There's is no reason why you can't learn how to foster and build a network from the ground up, and then make it a ritual in *your* daily life, the same as I have with mine. When you do, you'll experience countless rewards. Once you make it a habit, you'll wonder how you ever lived without consciously networking all the time. It's addictive – hopefully the best – or better yet the *only* – addiction you'll ever have.

In my own networktraining session, I put forth, in my training sessions, some basic management techniques that are essential to networking. Anyone can apply them. It doesn't take a Ph.D, or any degree at all, for that matter, to become an effective networker – just basic awareness of the process, application and practice.

You *can* network more effectively. Don't be duped into thinking that it's too tough or that you're just not outgoing enough to swing it. I know for a fact that *everyone*, no matter what his or her level of education or predisposition, can learn to network.

Why do it?

Without networking, you'll have a much more difficult time finding a job, locating the perfect house, hiring the right employee, attracting the right partner or spouse, acquiring new clients, making a sale, or just about anything else you set out to do in life.

Perhaps you've wondered:

"Why am I never asked to do this or that?" My response: Do you wait or do you create your own opportunities?

"Where can I find new markets?" My response: Anywhere and everywhere that people meet.

"How do I gather valuable information?" My response: Do you want the short or the long route? Networking will cut your time and effort in half.

As you know, today's marketplace is fiercely competitive. You can be as street smart and book smart as they come, but if you don't know how to connect with other people, no amount of diplomas, degrees or savvy will pave your way. Networking will.

My own story

Take me, for instance. I basically grew up on the streets. Sure, I had a warm, cozy, Italian/Irish-American family with five brothers and four sisters, but I also had a reputation to howl. I knew my way forward and backward through the rough and rowdy web of my neighborhood that I traversed with my best friend, Robert "Ikey" Carroll, a fellow Irish-American who still laughs about our antics – the basis, he insists, upon which I later built my networking business. Because I had friends and contacts throughout the various subcultures of my terrain, I could go anywhere and be accepted. From an early age, I recognized the power of a network, and I used it, even in my naïve youth, to get me both in and out of trouble.

You see, the "Ruf", as I came to be known, was truly a ruffian. "Trouble" wasn't only my middle name, it was my mantra. In fact, if I hadn't been prodded into joining the U.S. military by my older brothers, Robert ("Olo" to me) who had just returned from Vietnam, and , Joseph, who was serving in the U.S. Air Force in Japan, I guarantee that I'd probably be either in jail or dead today – despite the safety network I had engendered. Although I realize now that everyone is responsible for what he or she does and does *not* do, regardless of the power of a network, you couldn't have convinced me of that back then.

Irresponsible as I was, I skipped school a lot as a kid, and literally got my high school diploma by default. It didn't help, of course, that when I was 14 and 15 years old I worked evenings in an Italian pizzeria and then for a Jewish bakery from 1:00-3:00 AM stocking their delivery trucks, with school bidding unsuccessfully for my time in the space of a few hours.

Granted, my parents tried to drill discipline into me at home, but it didn't entirely work. The only discipline I employed was on the street where following the rules and knowing whom to energize to "get the job done" – whatever that was at the time – was clearly critical. I also learned the hard way that you don't tarnish your network, no matter what, and that holds true in every aspect of my life today.

Far from being complicated, networking is based on very basic concepts such as those. In fact, the rudimentary elements of networking that I had witnessed and used at home – such like visiting my Godmother, Aunt Louise Rothrauff, at the "5 and 10-cent" store where she worked, and getting free candy and attention – were the basis of my lifelong conditioning and devotion to networking.

"Order what you want," she'd say, as I settled myself in at the shop's lunch booth," and I'll be right back."

In the meantime, everyone who knew and worked with Aunt Louise would stop by to say hello, making me feel like a king, Fortunately, I wasn't too naïve at the time to realize the power of her network.

The same thing happened on the street. No matter where I went, people would ask me, instantly recognizing that I was Italian, if I was a Ruffolo, a Garritino or a Sorrentino. Once I replied that I was a Ruffolo, they would ask if I was Uffo's, Fuzzy's, Mundo's, Alfonso's, Jumbo's or Joe's kid.

"Joe's kid," I would proudly reply, and they would immediately invite me in to have something to eat and drink.

"Pretty cool, this network," quick-learner-that-I-was would think. "These connections make a difference."

Another person with connections all over town was my mother, Clara E., by far the best networker I have ever known. No matter where I was or how late it was, my mother knew how to find me. I remember that we were once at someone's house, very late in the evening and the phone rang. I heard Ikey's girlfriend say, "It's for you," and I was shocked because I thought no one knew I was there. Yes, Clara E., my mother, just wanted to know where I was and if everything was all right. Everyone looked at me, and Ikey said, 'Your mother *always* knows where you are."

Another time we went all-night bowling, not informing my parents, of course, but sure enough at around 3:30 AM the phone rang and someone asked, 'Is there a Ruffolo in the house?" and I said, "That's me." Guess who it was? Yes, Clara E., my mother. Again, she was just checking to dertemine where I was and to ensure that everything was fine. At the time, I did not understand what networking was but I knew, as well as my friends, the ability of my mother's networking skills. She had a powerful network and she could very effectively energize it to find her last-born son.

The street, then, was my "Basic Training" and the military my "Advance Training".

Fortunately for me (and my family), the military succeeded in finishing off the discipline that my parents and family tried to instill in me. In fact, had it not been for the U.S. Army, where a quick and thorough lesson in discipline turned into a 20-year military career, I never may have got the education I needed, provided free of charge, no less, while I was a soldier and Non-Commissioned Officer (NCO) stationed in Europe during 19 of those years.

Street smart? You bet. Book smart? I've got my AS (Associates Degree), my BS (I know what some of you are thinking, but it's a Bachelors of Science), and my MPA (Masters of Public Administration). It took me over 15 years of night school to get those degrees, but they wouldn't be worth two cents - whether dollars or euros - if I hadn't also learned how to network.

It was the military, in fact, that gave me my first lesson in networking, albeit in a rather crude way. Their *modus operandi* was "Kick butt and take names." I've toned that down a bit, you'll be glad to know, in my current work as a Professional Networker, Trainer, Speaker, Author and Publisher. I now shake hands and take names – but still in gun-powder time. In a split second, you learn who can do what for you, and vice versa. That's networking, pure and simple. From day one, the U.S. Army taught me to get focused and let others know what you want in record time, to "shoot, move and communicate" – or die -. The ultimate goal, of course, was to survive on the battlefield and return home to your family.

Networking is exactly the same. By finding out, *before* the opportunity and the moment pass, who has the resources you need, as well as who needs the resources that *you* have to offer, you connect for success. Mission accomplished.

You won't know what those resources are, however, until you tap into the well of your network.

Let your network do the walking

Let's face it, you can't rely solely on the Yellow Pages of the local phonebook to get you through life. You need connections. Real life connections. You need a network. And the sooner you realize this and build a network, the quicker you'll accomplish things, and the more fruitful and rewarding your life will be, not only for you, but for everyone who crosses your path.

With networking, opportunities are endless. One and one *will* equal four. You *will* find the resources you need and energize them to grow serendipitously for you.

Networking provides you with an edge. It's the difference between being plugged in or left out. It's the universal language of success.

For the skeptics

No doubt, some of you will be skeptical or critical. There are those who think that networking is nothing more than schmoozing to get what you want, whether it is money or favors.

To those I say, networking can clearly help you make more money, if that is your intent. We all have to earn a living (although some of us tend tothink that we need more money than is truly necessary). Financial reward, however, is only one facet of the multi-faceted benefits of networking. So, what are the others? Well, look at it this way. There isn't much that networking *can't* do.

Networking can help everyone, no matter what his or her status in life, to navigate the waters in a more productive, enriching way with less frustrations, bumps, and dead ends. It's not cheating, lying, or stealing. Networking is simply about using the connections you already make on a daily basis, and expanding those parameters by leaps and bounds to achieve your goals. The more you can feed that process, the more ease with which you'll travel through life and benefit others on your way.

Whatever your needs and wants are at any given time in your life - a new car, a new job, a new apartment, a new love, or something as simple as finding a good dentist, a lawyer, a financial advisor, a babysitter or even a puppy for your kids - networking can make it happen with the least amount of time, trouble and expense. Surveys show that networking is the number one way that people find jobs. I take that one step further and propose that it's the number one way to get *anything* accomplished in life.

You see, in *my* book, luck doesn't exist. I believe that successful people *make* their success happen; it doesn't just fall in their laps.

Success requires a combination of being in the right place at the right time, connecting with the right people, recognizing an opportunity when you see it, and then grasping it. That takes foresight, planning, resourcefulness, motivation, initiative, enthusiasm and gumption. After all, a key syllable in the word "networking" is "work". It's the paddle that moves the canoe. Without it, you're dead in the water.

As you'll learn more about in Chapter 9, there is another side to the equation as well: giving back. Networking is a give and receive process, not just take. My experience proves that if reciprocal good deeds are not spawned, the process falls flat and networking fails. It simply does not work if networking is one-sided. The scale must balanced.

So, no, networking cannot only be about what's in it for you. In order for it to work and last, networking must include a strong element of reciprocity. Case closed.

Networking as a way of life

The ultimate question is this: Why leave your network to chance if you can multiply your connections in life a million-fold by consciously and actively networking on a regular basis? Once you get the hang of it, you go into automatic pilot and networking becomes a habit, a way of life. Try it. You have nothing to lose, and everything to gain and give back.

If networking didn't work, I wouldn't be where I am today – a successful Professional Networker, Trainer, Speaker, Author and Publisher with an energized network of friends and associates around the world. Witness the comments throughout this book from people in every walk of life. They know beyond a shadow of a doubt that networking can be a productive, healthy, humanitarian way of life if properly learned and performed with good intentions.

The way I see it, there are two basic schools in life: the school of hard knocks and the art of networking, which facilitates almost anything you can imagine… and more. Why knock yourself out trying to make your life run smoothly when networking can ease the way? As sure as I know that my name is Charles Douglas Armando Ruffolo, that's how sure I am that networking will change your life.

ACN Executive Vouches for the Power of Networking

Art Napolitano knows all about the power of networking – after all, it's brought him from rags to riches – mega riches. Once a struggling musician, the only time he sings now is on his way back and forth to the bank, multi-millionaire that he is. As rising Senior Vice President and Circle of Champions member of ACN, a booming cooperative marketing company that provides telecommunications and energy products. Napolitano has experienced a wave of tremendous success based purely on networking and network marketing – the latter being an exponential form of marketing whereby network funnel and feed upon each other; and word of mouth is the language of success.

"In parallel with what Charles Ruffolo advocates with his fundamental networking premises," Napolitano confirms, "ACN has created a name and a client base through sheer word of mouth. As a result, in less than five years with the company, I personally have developed a team that has connected over a million telecommunications customers in 12 countries, with five new countries already slated for 2004."

"All of the principles that Ruffolo sets forth in his book, his training sessions and his The Network Club website, as well as his Giving Back Foundation philosophy, apply directly to my personal success and that of ACN. It is a credit to the concept and phenomenon of networking to say that, without one single dollar of advertising, we've surpassed our goals – in fact, we've completely blown them out of the water. Hands down, networking is the most lucrative way to do business."

Network marketing is such a powerful concept for moving products and services that in 1993, 14.9 million people were involved, and in 2002, that figure had risen to 46 million. Today, almost every product and service that you can think of is marketed through network marketing.

"Key to network marketing," Napolitano points out, "is the concept of residual income. Exponential market growth spawns automatically repetitive income, or residuals, as they are known. Building up a network – Ruffolo style - triggers the recurring stream of income, and the 'paid for life' premise comes into play. It only makes sense that network marketing is called 'the people's franchise,' for the people on the front lines truly benefit, over and over again."

"If it weren't for networking and the very principles that Ruffolo espouses," Napolitano insists, "I wouldn't be where I am today, providing a very good life for my wife, Jennifer, and our two children, and enabling us to keep a residence both in the United States and The Netherlands. Charles Ruffolo knows from whence he speaks. To say that 'networking works' is an understatement, and I vouch for that."

Art Napolitano
Senior Vice President
ACN Europe

Ruffolo's five basic principles of networking

At the core of all the networking training that I do are five basic requirements of any successful networking endeavor, upon which I will elaborate in this guide. In order to network effectively, you must:

1. *Begin your network.*
   This encompasses building and expanding your network. Discover the network you were born with, and how to take on the world from there.
2. *Know your network.*
   This involves communicating to and from your network. You'll be amazed at who's in it… and who else should be.
3. *Bond with your network.*
   This requires that you energize your network and share experiences. Put those parties and luncheons to work!
4. *Nurture your network.*
   This means you must lead your network, and follow certain proven methods for networking in action. For example, those articles you send to me about the Pittsburgh Steelers mean a lot! Find out what pushes *your* network buttons.
5. *Give to your network.*
   This demands that your network benefits from you in return. Giving back is so essential that I've declared it the cardinal rule of networking. Learn why and how to reciprocate.

Learning to network effectively

Despite its demonstrable power and effectiveness, networking is still, for many, a vague concept that is difficult to grasp. This book will show you exactly *how* to network by incorporating my practical methods and principles. When you've finished this book, you'll be able to go directly from "A" to "Z" without getting waylaid on "B" to "Y". You'll learn a skill that will set the pace for the rest of your life, and you'll be amazed at just how easy… and fun… networking can be. Best of all, it's free!

As I say on the cover of this book, *"Who you know is not as important as who knows YOU."* People must know in order to help you achieve your goals, and in order for you to help them achieve theirs in return.

Networking is the difference between watching and participating. You'll no longer need to ask yourself why you never receive whatever it is in life that you're seeking, because you'll be more self-confident and competent to achieve all of your goals, regardless of the extent, nature, or supposed difficulty.

In essence, you'll be a hundred times more productive and successful than you've ever been before.

"Everyone has the ability to network – it's not something you need to buy – but it is certainly something you need to learn, and requires a certain amount of motivation and the right tools to get you started. Charles Ruffolo provides that motivation and the right tools to get many people into networking who otherwise would not dare."

- Jennifer Wolf, VP European Operations
Akibia Consulting
The Netherlands

CHAPTER 2:

BUILDING YOUR NETWORK

"I come from a family of 10 kids – now that's a network! Today, my The Network Club alone has over 3,000 members, and my personal database over 15,000 names. So can yours."

- Charles Ruffolo, The NetworKing

Did you ever play "connect the dots" or "dot-to-dot"? It's a classic drawing game whereby you connect numbered dots in numerical order to create a picture. The same basic principle applies to building your network.

Networking is a matter of connecting the dots of your life and seeing where they lead. There are literally as many connections out there as there are numbers – infinite.

Number one is your home base, where all networking begins. After that, you're on a roll, but unlike the picture game, there is no finite end to networking. The picture evolves with each day and each interaction that you make.

As with the picture game, however, unless you intentionally move your pencil from one dot to another, it "ain't gonna happen." In order to build your network, you've got to make a concerted effort to play the game, seeking one connection after another rather than leaving it up to whim. The good thing is that you have a clean slate everyday with enormous potential. Get the picture?

Before you begin to draw upon and build your network, though, you've got to have a clear outline of your goals.

Everything from that point on is art – the art of networking.

Naming your passion or need

Your networking journey begins with a stated goal and a clear objective. Don't make it complicated. Just think about exactly what it is that you want to achieve at this point in your life. If you're like most people, you probably have more than one goal – immediate and long-term ones, big dreams and small ones. How many of them seem impossible or out of reach? They're not… not if networking is a regular feature of your life.

Is your goal to make a certain amount of money? To have a job that you really enjoy – not to mention one that's lucrative? To find a house in a better neighborhood, or perhaps one that's bigger… or maybe smaller now that you're an "empty nester"? To meet some new friends or, better yet, a new love?

Perhaps you're unemployed at the moment and desperately need to find a job. Any clue as to what your most important asset is?

Precisely. Your network.

Or maybe you have loftier ambitions. Do you want to increase your client or customer base, increase sales for your own company or your employer, or enhance relationships with existing customers? You clearly need a networking tactic, but first you have to identify your specific goal.

Chances are that you also have a healthy serving of even simpler agendas on your plate. Are you hankering for a new sofa for that living room or, more urgently, do you need a new washing machine? Perhaps you've moved to a different neighborhood or town and need to choose a new school for your child. Maybe you need to locate a doctor or hire a lawyer for that threatening divorce. Or maybe, on a more positive note, you simply need to find that bichon frise puppy for your child's next birthday. Perhaps you just need to locate a friend who lives in the city and you don't know how to get in touch with him or her, or you'd like to get tickets to an upcoming sporting event or concert.

Where do you start? Who do you call? Where do you go? Who can you trust? What resources do you tap?

Life can be daunting… without networking, that is. If you approach it with a goal in mind and formulate a plan – a networking plan – the pieces will fall into place. You can get through life much more smoothly, with less hassle, wasted time, cost and turbulence if you build a network and utilize it – regardless of your goals.

The NetworKing's 8P Principle

In my training sessions, I present the following The NetworKing's 8P Principle, a very straightforward illustration.

Characteristics of Planning Principle

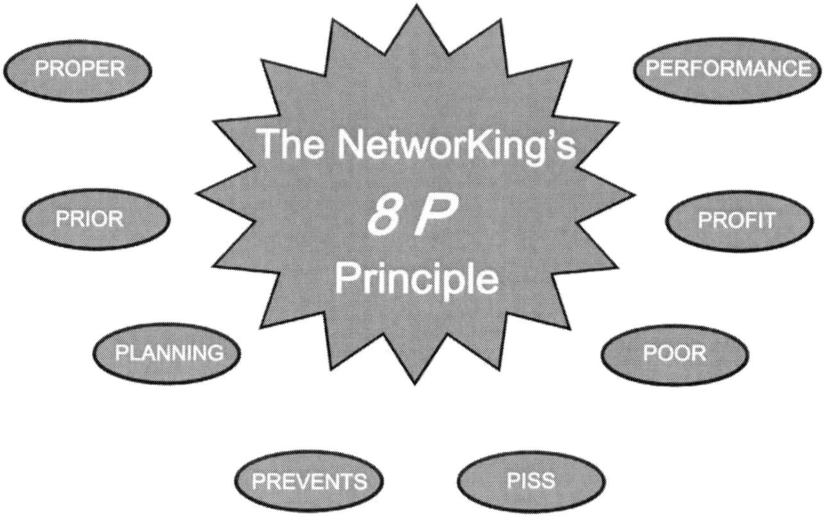

Proper Prior Planning Prevents Piss Poor Profit Performance

Use this principle to apply to your business or to your life in general as you set about to build your network. It applies equally. Without proper planning, which includes goal setting and identifying and targeting your resources, you'll be spinning your wheels. With my The NetworKing's 8P Principle, you'll be on the road to building your network in no time.

Think about your current goals. Where do you think is the best place to start building your network?

Networking begins at home

There may be "50 ways to leave your lover", thanks to songwriter/singer Paul Simon, but there are just as many, if not more, ways to build your network.

The most obvious one is to start with the silver spoon that you were born with – your family network. The moment you came into this life, you inherited an extended family. Have you considered the multitude of resources that they represent? Look closely at your relatives. Do you *really* know them? Whether you're fond of them or not, your extended family comes built in with a wealth of professions, skills, talents and contacts—resources all worth tapping.

Uncle John is a lawyer in town. Chances are that he knows a good divorce attorney, if that's what you need. While you're asking, you find out that Aunt Mary, his wife, has just convinced him to completely redecorate their suffering-sixties living room. As owner of the local interior decoration firm, would you like the first shot at the job?

Neighbor Bob is on the local city council. Wouldn't he be a likely source for a job opening in town? When you contact him, you further discover that he was just thinking about an after-school job for your daughter involving some part-time help at his art gallery. Perhaps she might be interested.

Aunt Jeannie manages a pet shop. What are the chances that she might know where to get that bichon frise puppy? It should come as no surprise that she also knows a local groomer, and an obedience school for your wayward prodigy of canine persuasion.

What about your in-laws and their whole side of the family? In-laws get a bad rap, but they represent a whole separate network. Perhaps you should look skyward past any sour apples and build some relationships up there. Think of the untapped wealth of resources in that often-downplayed branch of your family.

Growing up in a close-knit family taught me that we had every type of profession and occupation right there at our very core. I remember my own Uncle Tony saying that we had one of everything in our family, from a banker and a lawyer to a nun and even someone serving time in jail. We had it all, and I only needed to tap into my familial network for whatever it was that I needed.

Chances are that your family is somewhat similar. Granted, you may not have someone serving time in prison, but their backgrounds and endeavors are probably just as varied as mine and, yes, there are likely a few skeletons in your barricaded closet as well. Your network is surely more wide and varied than you think.

Now consider, if you will, whom all your extended family knows – their colleagues, neighbors, distant relatives, friends and acquaintances… the list goes on.

Does the same thing work for business and the acquisition of new clients? Of course it does. "A" leads to "B" who knows "C", but hang on – "C" just had a meeting the other day with "D", and "D" insisted that "E" was in the market for…

Do you get the picture? Networking is an exponential dream. Your resource map will grow substantially if you encourage it. The webs you weave spawn other webs, and on… and on… and on. Networking has a snowball effect, and the magnitude of your network depends solely on how well you pad it and pave it.

Consider all your existing resources and tap into them. Start with your immediate family and go way, *way* beyond. You'll be amazed at the branches leading off from the core network that you already have.

Since networking begins at home, establish your goals, begin with who you are and where you're from. Take a look at the profiles of your relatives, and branch out from there.

My mother was one of twelve children, my father one of ten, and I too was one of ten. You can bet that, to this day, I still depend on all those contacts, and they all depend on me. The silver spoon of your familial network will feed you for the rest of your life.

Building upon your base

It has been said that the average person knows 600 people. Reflect on the contacts in your own life. Make a mental note of all your colleagues and mentors, both professionally and socially. Include your own neighbors, the shopkeepers in your town, the faculty and staff at your children's school, the people you meet at your golf club. Concentrate on recognizing and maintaining your existing network while preparing to build and establish your new one.

Now think about the "random" people you meet in your travels, whether on a trip to Hawaai or a trip to the supermarket. If you appreciate the power of networking, you'll come to realize that those people are, in fact, never random. It is my firm belief that we *all* have some connection. To find out what that connection is, you must build rapport with the people you meet – anywhere and everywhere.

My own story

That's precisely what I did when I formulated my own plan to leave the U.S. military while I was still young enough to go into business. My wife Herma and I wanted to settle in The Netherlands where she was born and grew up, and where we met, so I needed a long-range plan to establish my base there in four years time when I was due to retire from the military. Even though I was an American soldier statioined in Germany at the time, my initial target audience, the American Chamber of Commerce (AmCham) in The Netherlands, gave me the benefit of the doubt and accepted me as a member in their relatively selective organization. Most likely, they figured that if I was perceptive enough and forward-thinking enough to aspire to being a member of their organization four years down the road, then I must have good business sense.

The point was that I had a goal. Various motivations led me to reach that goal – and my success rate depended primarily on how I networked in The Netherlands – despite a five-hour distance from my base in Germany! Strategic planning paid off.

Acceptance into the "AmCham" in 1991 was my first foray into the business world. Knowing that this members-only group was home to a broad range of American companies on Dutch soil, I ventured that they were the place for me to get involved. I was positive that AmCham would provide me with a wealth of networking opportunities. As soon as I could, I began attending their meetings and special events, networking in full force to build my network.

With the list of American companies in The Netherlands that I obtained from AmCham, I began to network intensively. I immediately set my sights on forty or more companies, from my home state of Pennsylvania, that were also based in Holland. I then identified those from Pittsburgh, my hometown – such as Heinz, PPG Industries, and so on. I was using a basic rule of networking: finding commonalities or links. Connecting with Pittsburgh companies was an obvious starting point. At the very least, it was a conversation starter. Further connections were bound to evolve from that connection.

Next step was to ask my wife Herma to look at a map of Holland and pinpoint where she'd like to settle. At her suggestion, we chose the idyllic countryside of the province of Drenthe, my wife's home turf after moving from Zeist in the center of The Netherlands. (By the way, I have a military link with Herma's father and sister – her father retired as an Officer after thirty-five years in the Dutch military service, and her sister, Wendy, is still in the Dutch military serving as a Colonel.)

Within a month, I not only had won first place at the AmCham's annual golf tournament, but also the respect of the new business world I was entering. Networking is powerful, indeed. Buford Alexander, then President of the American Chamber of Commerce in The Netherlands, a Harvard graduate and ex-military (U.S.) presented me with the trophy, and the rest is networking history. Today, Buford serves on the board of my Giving Back Foundation and a great friend and mentor to me.

The following year, I would pass the AmCham golf trophy onto Rupprect Quietch, who had just arrived in Holland from New York and was the General Manager of the Marriott Hotel. Again, that mere connection has grown into a long-distance network relationship as he has moved with his family to Prague, the Czech Republic and Berlin.

As a further way of building my network, I offered to help AmCham bring in new members by volunteering to help out with their membership committee. By promoting the benefits of AmCham to potential members and interacting with incoming ones, I would have first-hand access to a cache of companies. Clearly, it would bring me into contact with a vast network of potential employers and/or clients, depending on whether I started my own business or worked for someone else. The next dot on my networking picture had been connected.

Shortly thereafter, I was asked to sit on AmCham's membership committee in an official capacity. I was clearly in the right place at the right time, due to planning and initiative. I don't think I need to tell you how vastly effective this position was for my future. The benefits poured in. In fact, they were so rewarding that I'm still on that membership committee today.

Think about such committees where you could build your *own* network. It's a great way to volunteer and give back, and the outpouring of connections is incomparable.

As networking goes, I was recommended by someone in AmCham to the board of another related organization, the Amsterdam American Business Club (AABC), which was looking for someone to handle special events for them, also on a volunteer basis - another superb outlet and inlet for networking. Of course I agreed, without hesitation, and today, I serve as AABC's President.

Throughout this entire process, my motivation, enthusiasm and leadership played a major role. How I communicated my desires was equally critical. How I energized my network was key. These important concepts are all part of the overall dynamics of networking that we will cover throughout this book.

Based on my foresight, planning, initiative and determination, I had built a vital network. Above all, I had built that crucial element of *rapport*.

Building rapport

Once you've pinpointed your life strategy and determined who might be able to help you, the next step is to build rapport with that person of persons. Remember, to reach your goals, you'll need to reach out to those who relate to your needs. The people you need to reach are not going to second-guess your needs and come to you. You must plant the first seed by initiating the contact. It starts with a one-on-one contact, and develops into a long-term relationship.

Over time, rapport is built over time on a sense of respect, faith and trust. These basic values are the most important aspect of networking interactions since they allow you to bond with the other party in the most positive way. Somewhere in your repertoire you must possess some basic values that cause others to respect, admire and trust you. You must demonstrate that you will never breach their confidence, that you will be honest, and that you have *their* self-interest in mind.

Granted, it's often difficult to build upon a network without focusing heavily on what's in it for you, but it is necessary. Sure, networking brings people into your life that could be of great help to you in reaching your goals – that's one important side of the equation – but if you turn the focus outward, you'll find, as I have, that the results are far greater and certainly more rewarding.

Put yourself in the other person's place. Have you ever tried bonding with someone who doesn't respect you? It doesn't work. You wouldn't hire or work with someone that *you* didn't trust, so why expect others to do so? Think of someone you know that's unreliable. Would you want that person protecting your back in a dark alley? Use the "do unto others" doctrine, peppered with a strong infusion of courtesy. It really does make a difference.

In fact, the combination of trust, faith and respect is the *only* way to build rapport. If these ingredients are missing, you'll have to throw out the stew. Don't waste your time or someone else's time by being unreliable, untrustworthy and unfaithful. It will poison your network – or just about anything else, for that matter, that you set out to do in your life.

Use whatever means you have at your disposal to build rapport and, therefore, to build your network. Realize, however, that a full spectrum of *communication* skills is essential for networking.

Let's delve into that now.

"Ruf convinced me that my little book of contacts was not the main focus of my consulting business. Instead, I had to make sure that other people added my name and contact details to THEIR address books. That means radiating trust, and implies that you must take networking seriously. There is never a second chance to make that first impression."

Jonathan Marks, Creative Director
Creative Media Consultants
The Netherlands

CHAPTER 3:

COMMUNICATING TO YOUR NETWORK

"There's probably no greater compliment that one person can pay to another than the simple act of remembering something about that other person."

- Charles Ruffolo, The NetworKing

A large percentage of people have trouble communicating effectively. We're not talking about writing the great American novel or being an advertising executive. We're talking about good old-fashioned talking, particularly to strangers. And guess what? If you're now on a high about networking, you have no choice but to learn to communicate with strangers.

Again, it's not rocket science, although for many of you, it may feel like it is. The good news is that you're not alone. If I had to identify the number one roadblock that my friends and business relations have against being able to successfully network, it would be that they just don't know how to communicate effectively. So join the club and read on. And even if you're not in this club, read on anyhow, for I have a lot of hints as to how you can communicate better even if "running at the mouth" is easy for you. If that motor of yours is always charged, you're just one step ahead of the game.

Doing what comes naturally… or not

Although we all network in basic ways, why is it that some people are natural networkers while others find it prohibitively daunting? Which category are you in, or are you, like most people, somewhere in between?

Everyone, of course, has a different persona and a different way of approaching other people. If you have a more outgoing personality, networking most likely will come easier to you. On the other hand, just because you have "the gift of gab" doesn't mean that you're necessarily a good listener, and therefore, a good networker, but you do have a head start over someone who finds it difficult to generate a conversation.

Lack of effective communications skills is a primarily stumbling block for many people intent on networking. If you can't connect verbally with someone, how will you find out what links the two of you and what resources you can tap from each other? You can't. You've got to learn to communicate.

Again, it doesn't take a university degree in communications to get you going. With some simple skills set out here, you can make an enormous difference in your ability to *communicate* to your network for results.

No matter how you say it

In the end, in order to connect with someone and build rapport, you do need to communicate. Notice that I didn't say you have to be prepared to give a four-hour lecture. Just talk. In my training sessions and network event presentations, I use the sign language example below, which says 'Ruf Networker," to bring home the point that there are many ways to communicate to your network. In my opinion, there is no such thing as small talk; everything you say is important for networking.

No doubt, we communicate the whole day, every day. So why is it easy for one person while for others the art of conversation is an enormous nuisance, strain and dilemma?

Do you have difficulty speaking to someone you just met? Do you feel uncomfortable entering a conference of convention room because you may not know anyone and won't know what to say to those you don't? Do you sit at luncheons and wonder what to say to the person next to you? Do you worry about saying the wrong thing? Do you hesitate to ask for what you need or want?

Have you ever felt out of place moving into a new school, job or organization, not knowing what to say to whom? What about the same situation when you've joined a new sports club, or arrived at a party where you know no one but the friend or colleague that invited you? Do you enter a deadlock zone?

Obviously, such insecurities put you in a compromised position to network. In fact, poor communications is cited as the most frequent source of interpersonal conflict, so you can only imagine how it impedes networking. It literally gums up the works.

Whether you're a mom or dad trying to communicate with your rebellious teenager or an executive trying to communicate with insubordinate management, meaningful conversation is an effective art. And depending on your agenda for any particular day, some variation on the act of putting sentences together is called for in order to make an impact on another human being, and to be able to receive incoming messages as well.

Some of us are good at math, some at words and the connotations derived from words. There are tomes written on effective communications, but right now a tome is not necessary. All you need is this chapter, and the realization that you *can*, with some very basic premises, make a difference in how you communicate and intereact with others. Otherwise, you really can't network.

Effective networkers are master conversationalists. As a Professional Networker, it's my mission in life to network with everyone with whom I come in contact. That includes everyone from the doorman, busboy and janitor to the flight attendant, fisherman, diplomat, student, corporate CEO, celebrity and homeless person on the street. I talk to everyone in my path. And you know what? They talk back to me.

I've built my own brand of success on this very premise, and so can you. All you have to do is learn how to start a conversation and connect.

However, don't mistakenly think that you should only converse with those who appear to have something in common with you, of those who can benefit you. Set your priorities, of course, to meet the pressing needs you have, but don't overlook the serendipitous results of talking to *everyone* you meet. You'll soon realize that good things come out of every encounter, and that conversation is the key to finding the links in your life.

Where is this going to get me?

You may be Einstein's prodigy, but if you can't get your ideas across to someone else, you're missions are doomed. Likewise, if you can't promote yourself or even make casual conversation in a social or business setting, you'll be missing out on the vast network out there just waiting to be tapped. You also won't discover how to reach out and give back if you can't connect with what other people need

Let's face it, it's difficult to find a woman or man to go out on a date if you don't network! Finding the right person to ask is the obvious first step. Figuring out how to ask him or her is the next. Networking – and the art of communications – can facilitate even your love life.

Indeed, whatever your status and goals in life at any given time – whether you're unemployed and looking for a job or wanting to expand your business internationally – your effectiveness depends on your ability to communicate. Good communications is necessary in both your daily life and your work so that:

- you can speak the language of success
- you can hold your own with the best
- you can win with your words
- you can talk your way to the top.

It is not as difficult as you may think.

Five easy steps

Communications is the process whereby verbal and non-verbal information is sent and received, as shown in the illustration below. It's simple as that… or is it? Well, not if you have trouble sending and receiving.

The Communication Process

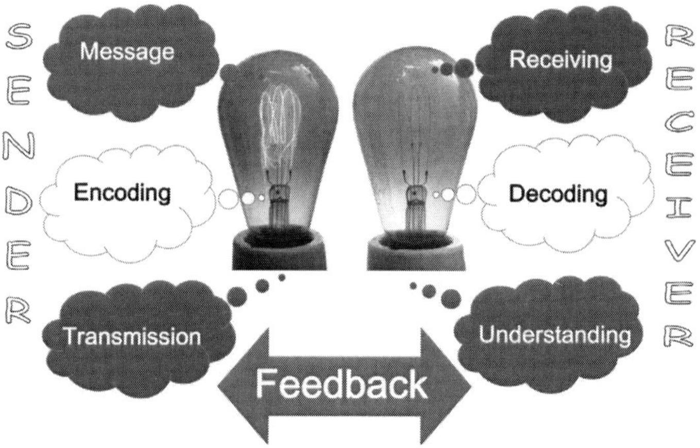

In order to send and receive a clear message, you must polish your communications skills so that you send and receive messages accurately and specifically, stating your message as simply as possible by using the right language, without hidden meanings. Body language is important as well. if your body is slumped over, for example, the message will come across loud and clear that you're not interested – or, for that matter, interesting.

Effective communications also means listening to what the other person is saying, how it is said, and what the other person does *not* say. Listen for that as well, and you'll be amazed at what you don't hear. It can tell you just as much about a person as what you *do* hear. In a perfect world, perfect communications would exist when the receiver perceived a mere mental picture envisioned by a sender – in essence, mental telepathy. That's not what we're attempting here, but you can approximate the effect with good, solid communications.

Essentially, there are two kinds of communications: one-way and two-way. One-way involves information flowing downhill, such as memos, or lectures, e-mails, written instructions and mass media. Two-way communications is what networking is all about. You can't network through one-way communications. Networking requires that you foster reciprocal communications whereby information flows back and forth and mutual understanding takes place. Some obvious examples are telephone conversations, question and answer sessions, discussions and debates and, in short, responding to the communications you receive and vice versa. After all, your network won't work unless the receiver on the other end takes hold. Effective communication facilitates that process.

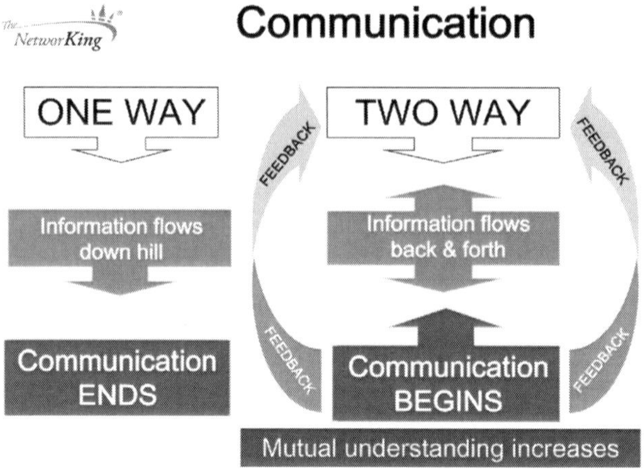

In order to communicate to your network, you must follow these five easy steps for effective two-way communications:

1. Build a rapport with your network before you communicate.
2. Seek similarities or commonalities.
3. Know what you'll say.
4. Know who your audience is.
5. Listen to your network.

Communicating with a handshake

Don't be fooled into thinking that a handshake is just a handshake. Far from it. The same way that eye contact tells a lot about your interest and confidence, i.e. the more direct, the more interested and confident you appear, handshakes reveal more than many of us realize. So why not learn to adapt and perfect this simple gesture for enhanced communications? It certainly doesn't take much effort.

While a firm handshake works well for the general public (no one likes a limp handshake), there are times when I admit to adapting my handshake for a particular audience. For example, when I'm introduced to my nephew's friends in school or giving a networking session to high-school kids or university students, I always communicate quickly in the language that gets their attention – a carryover from my days as a ruffian in Pittsburgh – by using what I refer to as a more active, youth handshake involving several rapid movements, and ending by hitting my fist or hand to my chest. Young people are often more receptive to this handshake, as it helps to easy our initial strangeness and their often alleviates their frequent "I refuse to relate to this uncool adult" attitude. I communicate with them in their own language, and they usually find it "hip" or "in", or at the least, a bit fun instead of stodgy. What really surprises them is to see me using that same handshake with their parents. What they forget is that we codgers invented that handshake!

In the military, we also learned to communicate with our hands, but in this case certain gestures meant that the enemy was near. Sometimes no words are necessary.

Lesson? Adapt, learn to recognize what works when, and use it.

Building rapport through dialogue

In order to network properly, it's critical to plan for networking by determining your strategy, i.e. what you want to accomplish, and then building a rapport with the people in your potential network. In order to move ahead in life, you need to be able to communicate to your network, be it friends, family, your colleagues or your boss.

The quickest and most effective way to build rapport with someone is through dialogue. In general, you need to plan, find and talk about common interests to encourage the flow of communication. Click on that embedded software in your head and find topics to talk about.

You could begin, for example, by talking about the weather, a rather boring, cliché way to begin, but nonetheless a beginning. You could talk about the traffic jam you were just in, or the keynote speaker for the convention you happen to be attending, or even your client's office furnishings. Look around you and hone in on something that catches your eye about the other person, whether it be the snapshot of his dog – which happens to be the same breed as yours – or the moose head on the wall just begging for comment. (After all, it wasn't hung there to be inconspicuous.) Talk about current events or the book on his or her desk that you've also read; comment on the music playing – didn't you just buy that CD? Discuss a movie you saw last night or the sports event you went to. Use newspaper stories or your own experiences as overtures.

Common experience is also a good conversation starter. You might discuss the venue you happen to be attending, or the organization or cause which brings you both to the same place, or the game you watched last night. Seek similarities and commonalities. Find the common thread.

A very simple example from my own youth involves moving and growing up "on the streets". By the age of 14, we had moved over ten times. I say over ten instead of an exact number, because I can't even remember beyond that. It became a blur.

What I do remember is how difficult it was to re-invent the wheel and establish my turf in a new neighborhood so often … perhaps that's why I network with such ease. I had lots of practice at a very young age. What I essentially did was to transport my "network", that is my adopted buzzwords, talents and interests, along with me as an entrée to new territory. The first thing I'd do when we arrived was to find a place where I could play "hoops", or basketball. It didn't take me long to figure out that any pick-up game of sports - be it basketball, football or baseball – was one of the quickest ways for a new kid on the block to build a new network.

That was just the beginning though. After the games, we would talk about our favorite sports figures and what we would have done if we were in their shoes and, of course, what we'd do with all their money. We would also talk about where we came from and whom we knew… all the while building rapport and a sense of new belonging through communications. We didn't realize at the time that we were networking, but we were. And I got fairly adept at breaking into unfamiliar territory in record time. It wasn't long before the neighbourhood kids accepted me into their network and were asking me to hang out with them on the 4th Street corner. Next thing I knew, my brother Bobby was having a party in Oakland, PA, and I asked if my new friends could come. By doing so, I connected those two networks, and it not only grew for me but also doubled for all those involved.

If you follow this networking track, you'll realize, as I do now, that I was utilizing the entire networking process: beginning, getting to know, communicating to, bonding with, nurturing and giving back to my network. Now… think about how often you do this in your own life. It doesn't matter whether you're on the street or in the boardroom. The same principles apply. Learn what your network wants to hear, and what you have to share with them; communicate that, and rapport will follow.

You can also discuss viewpoints – everyone has one. Just be careful to respect the boundaries here, both culturally and politically. A battle is certainly not rapport. It is a fact, however, that the more intense the interaction, the more you will be remembered. Just be sure you're remembered for being polite and civil as well as for your opinions. Don't tread on dangerous territory. There are certainly enough safe subjects and approaches to lean on. If the common nerve you hit is a bleeding artery, chances are you won't see that person in your network again. If that happens, be prepared to regroup and try using a different approach. Those bridges you burn could be mighty hard to cross again.

Learn to listen for clues. Draw out from the other person his or her interests, and capitalize on the similarities to your life. Get people talking about themselves. Most people love the limelight; let it shine on them. Then file away those facts and retrieve them the next time you meet. Remembering key things about other people is the greatest compliment you can pay.

Find a link, a bond, a common denominator, and talk about it, however briefly. It may seem trivial, but these are conversation starters, like hors d'oeuvres to a good meal. They open the appetite for more discussion and make the other person feel at ease. It doesn't have to be painful. You are simply building rapport.

Some examples of introduction ice-melters might be:

- Have you been here before?
- Are you a member of this organization?
- Are you a golfer?
- That tie you're wearing is great! Was it a gift?
- Isn't this décor stunning?
- Have you heard this speaker before?
- I noticed that you're reading… Have you read her latest book…?

If you truly can't find anything to talk about, just ask to pass the salt. Then talk about the taste of the food, or the lack thereof. Breaking the ice is the first step, wether to do with sports interior decoration or plain salt. Rest assured that the more you practice rapport building through communications, the more fluid your conversation will be in the future, and the quicker your networking will become a breeze. Just remember that if you begin to talk about something that appears to aggravate someone, smooth over the bump because no one should be slighted or insulted.

As I've said before, it is my firm conviction that everyone has a connection to your life. Make it your mission to discover what that connection is. It can actually be quite an enjoyable challenge, and a perfect way to communicate for success.

Brushing up on your interpersonal skills

How you come across or communicate to your network is as important as whether your shirt-tail is sticking out of your slip is showing. If you have trouble in this area, here are a few hints:

- Treat prospective clients as if you already know them.
- Don't be effusive, but do be friendly. No one likes a stiff.
- Share a bit about yourself to give something to build on.
- Dont't be arrogant. Be approachable.
- Be respectful to others.
- Develop rapport. Bring with you a common bond, and find others as you talk.
- Make a friend. Much business is, like it or not, based on friendship and cronies. The quickest way to do business is to befriend someone. It's a fact of life that we all do business with people we like. Think about it.
- Build trust. If you can't be trusted and relied upon, your networking will be pointless.

In essence, know your audience. If you don't, someone else will.

The icing on the cake

Developing good communication skills can enhance and help you to:

- Lift moral (your own and others)
- Show you care.
- Understand yourself better.
- Inspire and motivate others.
- Demonstrate solidarity among others.
- Bring a smile to the face of someone.
- Get a good grasp of a situation.
- Display compassion, trust and inspiration.
- Engender confidence.

Isn't good communications worth all that and more? Networking is simply the by-product.

Building a networking bridge

Think of how you generally approach people. Are you abrupt, shy, or somewhere in between? Are you approachable or standoffish? Do you have trouble starting or maintaining a conversation with strangers, or even with people you know fairly well? Do you have a broad range of interests to talk about? Do you keep up with current events?

Think about your communications style. How do you think it could be improved?

Here are some further tools for getting started:

- Take the first step and initiate the conversation. Simply say hello.
- Maintain eye contact and smile. (If you wanted a date, your smile would be so big that you could eat a banana sideways! Smiling doesn't cost a thing. Try doing it more.)
- Encourage others to contribute to the conversation.
- Use humor appropriately to lighten the mood.
- Be well-read and familiar with current events to give you something to talk about.
- Have a broad range of interests.
- Put people at ease with your friendliness.
- Ask the opinions of others.
- Be open to change and exchange.
- Be enthusiastic.

In the subtle art of conversation, effective networkers have an attitude and a knack of caring about the other person, and it can be sensed instantly. You don't need to feign interest in another person if you learn to foster genuine interest. There is always something about another person that you can relate to; sometimes you just have to dig further to find it.

Here are a few questions to get you started:

- "What's your full name?" This simple knowledge, besides being critical for future reference, may spark some connection on which to hang your conversation. For example, perhaps the surname is coincidentally the same as someone from your ancestry, or the same as your friend's or neighbor's. Maybe the surname will indicate an obvious nationality to which you have a connection: "Spizzirri! You must be Italian. I lived in Cerisano in Italy for a year and….."

- "Who do you work for" or "Do you run your own business?"
- "What's your line of work?" Perhaps you work in the same or a similar field, or someone you know does. (People in some cultures have a difficult time breaching what they believe to be "privileged" information and, therefore, an invasion of privacy. I personally don't consider a person's career as something private, but perhaps you do. On the contrary, if a person wanted to hide a job, why would he or she be doing it? In my opinion, it's virtually impossible to network, at least in the business arena, if you are reluctant to discuss careers.)
- "What is your background, i.e. what brought you here?" Perhaps the person is an expatriate like your, and then the conversation really takes off.
- 'What do you like to do in your spare time?" Perhaps you both golf or like art history. Look for conversational links.

In short, ask the questions that the other person might enjoy answering and, above all, encourage people to talk about themselves. A lot of people have trouble doing this. If you're one of them, perhaps it's because you are a bit nervous, shy or insecure, and you tend to focus the conversation solely or primarily on you because you don't know what else to say, or you don't want to appear too forward by asking personal questions of the other party. Maybe you are just normally more self-focused. If so, remember to turn down the volume of your own glorification and turn your eyes, ears and full attention to the other person – with sincerity.

A dialogue isn't a dialogue unless there are two people speaking. Are you only hearing yourself? Adjust the output.

Characteristics of Listening Principle

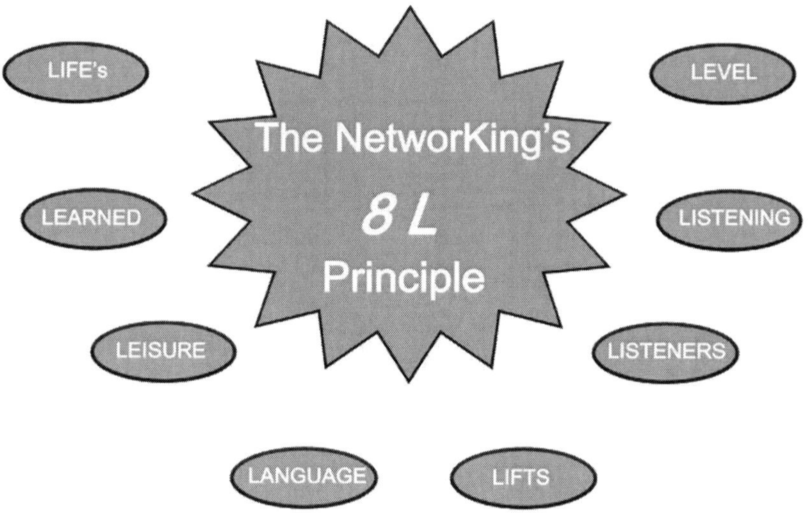

***Life's** Learned* ***Leisure** Language* ***Lifts** Listeners* ***Listening** Level*

If you tend to talk too much about yourself and control the conversation, practice dropping the "I" in your sentences and concentrating instead on the other person's interests and needs. Find out what matters to that person and, without exception, you will stumble across something you have in common. I guarantee it. At that point, you can bounce the conversation back and forth between the two of you, providing an opportunity for you to debut your flag as well. You are now in the process of networking for mutual benefit. Make it a game you'll both win.

Listen with your eyes as well as your ears. "Eye lock" is a powerful tool for interpersonal communications and, therefore, productive networking. Making and maintaining eye contact is one of the surest indicators that someone is tuning in and not out. If you look someone directly in the eyes as either of you speak, you will be amazed at how quickly you get a positive response or even a compliment. The look that you need to get the date, the job, the sale or simply the best seat in the house is not a downcast, backward, i.e. insecure look. Look in the eyes with confidence. Learn to communicate with your eyes as much as with your mouth.

Positioning your request

Eventually, after you've built a solid rapport, you've got to get around to asking for what you want or need. Relying on second-guessing is a lonely, futile game. When the moment is right, present your request. If you've taken the time to build your network, your communication must eventually address what it is that you need to achieve, and whether that person might be able to help. Be ready in the next breath, however, to offer equal or greater support in return.

Shaking the hand of a stranger and saying the first words is difficult for some people. Asking for what you need or want can be doubly difficult. My best investment in life was shaking the hand of a stranger in 1976 in a clothing boutique in Steenwijk, a small village in The Netherlands, near where I was stationed with the army. Her name was Herma Petronella Broesder, the woman I would marry four years later and the one that I'm still married to and banking on forever.

Here's how it evolved. In 1976 I was stationed in The Netherlands with the U.S. Army – one of many postings throughout Europe. Private Gene Fast from Minnesota, who was in my "outfit" or Army unit, asked me to go into town and help him shop for a shirt which he needed for a party. Walking into a little boutique, I saw a young lady with long dark hair past her waist and wearing a khaki shirt. She was "lookin' good". Real good.

I bet Gene five Guilders, the Dutch currency at that time (about $2.50 – hey, I was on a soldier's budget) that I would take her out, and the bet was on. Believe me, my network was energizing. No time to do research on her, unfortunately, but this cold call was definitely warming up. Our connection was that she needed to make a sale, and Gene needed a shirt. Maybe ten shirts.

I approached her, greeted her with a smile and a handshake, and introduced myself.

"Hello, Sergeant Ruffolo. Private Fast here needs to try on at least then shirts."

Obviously, the more shirts, the longer he would be in the dressing room and I could network.

"No, that one's not it," I would say to Gene every time he came out. "Try another one."

Quick on my feet that I am, I asked the target of my affection, "So, what does your boyfriend think about you working on Saturdays?"

"Oh, I don't have a boyfriend."

YES! It's open season.

"So, what do you do in your free time?"

"Well, for one thing, I sing in a Gospel group."

"Great! I also sing… in church."

Little did it matter that I sang with the rest of the congregation, not solo.

"Do you like pizza?" (My Italian heritage kicking in.)

"I've never had it."

"What? You've never had pizza? (I knew which side the mozzarella was on at this point.) Well, how 'bout if I take you out for a pizza sometime soon? Would you be willing to give me your name and phone number?"

Thirty-four years after the pizza, I still have that piece of paper and the love of my life… even though my wife is now well aware that I can't carry a tune. That stranger in the boutique turned into my best friend, my wife, my lover and my soul mate – thanks to Gene Fast from my military network… and a shirt. That five guilder bet I made was my best return on investment ever.

Remember, there are no strangers, only friends you have not met. So get out there, shake some hands and position yourself for success. The beauty of networking is that you never know where it will lead.

Crossing the networking bridge

As with anything in life, there are definite *turn-ons* and *turn-offs* in communications, some based on cultural differences and others based on common courtesy. Let's look at some of the ways in which you can both *turn on* or *turn* off positive vibes:

Turn-ons

- Honor people's time. Be bright, be brief, be gone.
- Smile and use humor.
- Tell amusing or engaging anecdotes.
- Listen, observe and study.
- Relax, share and have faith.
- Engage in eye contact.
- Enjoy life, and others will find you enjoyable.
- Remember that everyone has something to share. Don't hog the limelight; seek out others' interests and passions.
- Be courteous.

Turn-offs

- Touching when talking (Do this ONLY when you know it's appropriate;
- be aware of cultural protocol here.)
- Giving a lot of detail in casual conversation. Don't go overboard and tell your life story; skim the surface.
- Being intrusive. Don't be nosy and rude.
- Talking about touchy topics, e.g. religion, politics.
- Telling people they are wrong. Save your pedagogy.
- Eavesdropping and butting in. Respect boundaries and exhibit manners.
- Ignoring the space of others. Again, cultural protocol comes into play here. Respect your host country's unwritten rules of physical space between bodies when conversing. If you don't know what they are, find out.
- Glancing around the room while talking. Nothing is more of a turn-off than someone who's obviously more interested in anything and everything but your conversation.
- Forcing yourself on people. Respect limits. Learn to sense another's disinterest or decided annoyance with you, and walk away gracefully. If you've overstepped your boundaries, know when to back off and move on.

Remembering names

Remembering names is an art in itself, but there are subtle, simple ways to improve your score. Business cards and nametags play a very important role here.

Have you ever noticed how kids remember names? Whether it's sports players or Pokemon cards, if they keep talking about their favorite characters long enough, the names stick. They make them part of their network. With practice, you can do the same.

First of all, when you simply can't remember someone's name that you should know, there are a number of ways to bring about recall:

- Tell the truth. One approach is simply to say, "Remind me of your name again…", admitting that you have met before, but quite honestly can't remember the name. You could also say, "It's been one of those days. I certainly remember you, but could you please tell me your name again?"

- Ask the host or hostess.
- Ask for their business card – or another one if you've been given one before. Remember that a business card contains a lot of valuable data that you need anyhow, and that knowledge is power. Be prepared to hand out your business card as well.
- Read the business card. Look for conversation starters or links while you're at it. Business cards should prompt at least five or ten dialogues. Ex.: "Oh, I see you're from Friesland (a province in Holland). You must speak Frisian as well then…"; "I see that your name is the same as your business… are you the founder?"; "Your logo is very clever. Who designed it?", etc., etc.
- Associate the name with their company name.
- Match a name with a face. Notice distinguishing features.
- Extend your hand, say your name and listen for the other person's name. People respond in kind 90% of the time.
- Read his of her nametag.
- Repeat a person's name when you're introduced.
- Think about the person, and look at them as you say their name.
- Focus on the person, not on your next conversational tidbit.
- Think of someone else with the same name, and associate the new person with that familiar person.
- Do what you can to remember, but be forgiving of yourself and others.

On the subject of names, do you know who you were named after or what your name means? It's a great conversation link if your name holds some particular interest. For example, every part of my name has a link. I wasn't named Charles Douglas Armando Ruffolo for nothing. "Charles" comes from my mother's brother; "Armando" from my father's brother; "Douglas" from the fact that my mother liked Douglas Fairbanks, an actor; and, of course, "Ruffolo" as the family name which, interestingly enough, means "Fame Wolf" (hey, I didn't choose it, after all!). Think of all the potential conversations attached to names.

Business cards: The number one networking tool

Business cards are the most valuable networking tool at your disposable, and the cheapest way to market yourself. I can't tell you how many people come to my The Network Club events and seminars without business cards. More incredible is how many people don't even have them at all. I find this unbelievable. If you're inhibited or feel that it's too pushy to give out business cards, let's get one thing straight: business cards are designed for doing business, and anyone who expects to network should never be without them.

Whether you are a student, a mother of 12 kids or a corporate executive, you need to network, and you CANNOT network properly without a business card. A business card is the most important instrument you can use to communicate about yourself. It's a mini-reflection of you by which someone can remember and contact you. Regardless of what you do in life, business cards demonstrate, in a very convenient way, your thoughtfulness, dedication, commitment and purpose in life. They show that you have initiative. And what are employers looking for? All of the that.

Business cards place your future literally in the hands of someone else. They provide others with a direct means to distinguish you from others, including your competition. In a convenient format both for you and the recipient, they provide immediate access to who you are, what line of work you're in, where you're located and the various ways to reach you – precisely what you need to network. They are, or should be, as important an investment as your computer or your website – maybe more so.

Regardless of your status in life, everyone should have a business or calling card, whether you own a business, work for someone else, or are a stay-at-home mom or dad, a college student or a hot dog vendor on Park Avenue in New yourd. It's an invaluable way to communicate to your network, and one that is grossly underestimated and underutilized.

Your business card takes over where your birth announcement left off. My very first business card was my birth certificate, telling the world that at 5:32 PM on July 17th, 1957, Charles was born to Clara E. and Joseph P. Ruffolo in Braddock, PA.

Below is my wife Herma's birth card that her parents sent out to their network in The Netherlands:

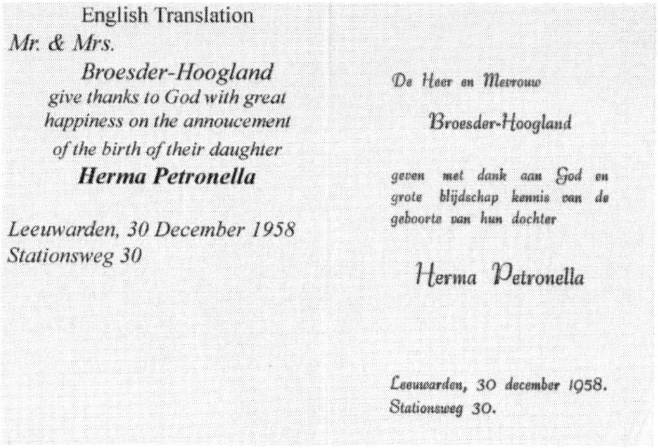
English Translation

Mr. & Mrs.

Broesder-Hoogland

give thanks to God with great happiness on the annoucement of the birth of their daughter

Herma Petronella

Leeuwarden, 30 December 1958
Stationsweg 30

De Heer en Mevrouw

Broesder-Hoogland

geven met dank aan God en grote blijdschap kennis van de geboorte van hun dochter

Herma Petronella

Leeuwarden, 30 december 1958.
Stationsweg 30.

Birthcards and announcemts are the forerunners of business cards

Business card savvy

Business cards must be designed tastefully, with the right wording, colors and graphics. A good graphic designer is worth his of her weight in gold when it comes to developing an appropriate logo or logotype for you. However, they can also be done very inexpensively; in fact, I've seen some very nice ones that were simply and quickly printed off the computer at a minimal cost.

In this day and age, your e-mail address is probably the most important piece of information that you can put on a business card, followed by your mobile or cellphone number, then your address (if desired) - particularly if you have a business - your home or business telephone number, and any website you may have. I personally regard the mobile or cellphone number as the key piece of information, as I like to have direct contact with whomever I'm calling, without any middleman or woman. I want to "breathe the same air" as the other person I'm trying to reach.

Some people like to keep their cellphone number private, but if you expect to network for success, you've got to be available to the masses at almost all times. Otherwise, you're cutting down your availability by about half. Sure, I turn mine off when I'm in a meeting or other important situation, but the rest of the time you can rest assured that I'm wired. If you do turn your phone off and someone leaves a message, it goes without saying that you should have the common courtesy to call him or her back at your earliest convenience. Who knows, it could just be the call that will make a difference in your – or someone else's – life. The way I look at it, a missed call is a missed network, and perhaps a missed opportunity to give back.

Also customary to include on your business cards is your professional title, which should be printed under your name. (If you don't have a designated title, come up with your own.) Decide whether educational designations, such as "MPA" or "MBA", should be included, depending on the culture in which you operate. Consider whether the mention of such diplomas has meaning for the particular audience that you're most often trying to reach.

In preparation for leaving my 20-year career with the U.S. military to transfer to civilian life, one of the first things I did was to have my own business cards printed, despite the fact that I had no particular business.

Here's what my first one looked like four years before leaving the military in 1995:

C.D.A. Ruffolo
U.S. Army

CEBNW,PSC 75
APO AE, 09719
05240-13399

Unit Address
Coevorden Kanaal 9
7741 PA Coevorden

That's all it says, but it was the replacement for my identification tag, or "dog tag" as the military calls these vital metal pieces worn around the neck, and just as important in communicating who I was and the fact that I wanted to be remembered.

On my current business cards, a sample of which you see below, I have my brother's name and business specialty on the reverse, even though he is based in the United States. Talk about networking! We are an ocean apart, but I'm still able to spread the word about him in such a simple, inexpensive way.

There are several reasons why I do this. Number one, I highly respect him and want to use every chance I can to network for him. He's the one who returned from Vietnam and told me to get off the streets and go in the military to find myself. Despite the fact that I insisted I knew who I was, he convinced me ... and I owe him, big time.

"Just go in for three years and use that time to get your education," he advised.

I stayed 20 years and retired with my Masters Degree, so he was right.

Secondly, I admired and wanted to emulate his later business success, so his name on the back of my card is a small gesture of thanks once I started my own company, following his example.

Finally, the fact that I have his U.S.-based business on the back of my card gives an even more international scope to my own business than I already have. Whether people need contacts in The Netherlands or the United States, my brother and I can handle it between the two of us. Further, it demonstrates to my brother and to my entire network some of the core values that I abide by –respect, family priority, honor, pride, and sharing the wealth by giving back.

You'd be amazed what you can learn from someone's business card. Again, that knowledge is power. Use it to kick-start your conversations and to make a physical or mental file of your contacts.

Ask anyone who knows me. I collect business cards like they were my last meal. Once back home in my office, I enter all the data from them into my computer data file, and toss most of the cards, except for those of prime importance that I carry with me. (If I used a PDA, that would be negligible. PDA's are a way to store the information as well, and are much more portable. I personally don't use one because too often they crash and I need information on my network at every moment, not tomorrow.)

With that in mind, let's look again at my own business card and consider what questions might be prompted.

How about these?

- What is a Professional Networker?
- What does MPA mean?
- What does The NetworKing stand for?
- Who is Ruf?
- What is the The Network Club?
- Is your name Italian?
- Why do you have two different addresses on your card?
- Where is Nijeveen?
- You have four names… are you Catholic?
- Is this your own company?
- Who is Robert A. Ruffolo?

Consider what information *your* card might transmit to others. Then be creative and think of how you can design your business or personal card. Don't be overly clever or tacky, however. This is a serious representation of you and your station in life, so make them your best advertisement possible. The important thing is that you do get them printed for yourself, and that you do hand them out as often as you can. In case you still don't get the full picture, suffice it to say that you need to print a lot of them.

If you don't have your own cards, read my lips: MAKE THEM AS SOON AS POSSIBLE! Then, always be prepared to hand them out to whomever you meet. As far as I am concerned, there is never any excuse for not having a card. I repeat, never. Trust me, you never know who you will meet on any given day.

And please, don't tell me that you never carry your business cards while on a holiday or vacation. Big mistake. Don't you think it's possible that the person next to whom you are camping or splashing in the pool may be a potential resource or business contact? Absolutely! Can you afford not to carry around this lightweight but super powerful tool? Absolutely not! Vacation or no vacation, make them readily accessible. They're the cheapest marketing tool there is and a sure-fire way to promote you to your en entire network.

Cold-calling should never be cold!

If you're livelihood depends on sales, "cold calls" are a way of life for you. Going to see a person that you've never met before with the prime purpose of selling a product or service can be quite inhibiting. Well, let me tell you something; it's inhibiting precisely because you're going in cold.

In my opinion, there should be only "warm calls". Cold calls seldom work well. Why? Because you have not taken the time to do your networking homework and find out about the person you're counting on for a sale. If you really want to get to first base in your business, find out something about the person before you meet. Not only will it be a more interesting conversation for both parties, but it will also be more productive. No one is going to hand you business on a platter without first connecting with you in some fashion.

In order to foster those connections, you must energize your network – before you meet – by doing some basic research. Ask around. Better yet, study the person's website. Find a hook or a connection from the information posted there for your benefit.

My partner in crime for this book, Shirley Agudo, did precisely that when she was looking to expand her writing and editing client base in The Netherlands where we both live. After checking Google and Ask Jeeves for PR agencies in The Netherlands, she began searching each of them for suitable matches. One particularly caught her eye, and she noticed that on that agency's client list - conveniently posted on the website to impress prospective clients – was the name of a company for whom she had worked full-time in the States.

An immediate connection was made - a powerful one at that, considering that she had worked in precisely the same public relations capacity for them as the agency now serves as consultant, moreover, as a full-time PR employee at the client's headquarters. Would she use that as her entrée to an interview? You bet! It worked like a charm. After "casually" mentioning this important connection on an initial phone call to the head of the agency, she was invited in for an interview, and secured them as a new client.

You could also employ a subtle, simple method that I use to link with key players. Find out who sits on the board of a particular charity or organization and then figure out a way to volunteer your time with that group and, ultimately, meet that person outside of their normal business setting. Use such means as a kickboard for connections, while giving back at the same time. There's nothing wrong, in my mind, in tapping the existing resources, regardless of where they are found. Cleverness and resourcefulness can serve you and your network well. It's the resourceful person who gets one step ahead of the crowd. Will you be the leader or the follower? The choice is yours.

Use whatever it takes, then, to connect, but connect in some way, shape or form. The challenge for you is to figure out how. But once you get in the routine of seeking links, you'll see how easy it is. The links are always there; it's your networking challenge to find them and utilize them.

Two magic words

Another invaluable networking tool that takes such little effort but goes a long way is the simple act of saying "thank you" to others for their efforts. Common courtesy in this way indicates to others, who have given you their time, attention, shoulder, ears or help, that you appreciate it. Everyone likes to be appreciated. When you take time to notice what others do for you in your network, they cannot help but notice you back.

Thank the host or hostess for inviting you, and specifically refer to something that you liked about the event or day for which he or she was responsible. Thank the waitress or waiter for his or her exceptional service; thank the organizer of an event for all his hard work to make it a success; and thank the keynote speaker for her viewpoint. Express thanks routinely. It takes less than one minute but can make such an impact on those on the receiving end.

Saying "thank you" is an easy way to reinforce your network and give back in a very small way. Get into the habit of doing it.

There are other ways to say "thank you" as well, of course. Companies can thank their clients in numerous ways – with invitations to sporting events, special parties or gatherings, with Christmas cards, etc. Whatever ways you choose are sure to be appreciated. Don't overlook this simple way to communicate and to maintain your image. It keeps your network alive.

Follow-up

It almost goes without saying that you need to follow up on your interactions. You've successfully communicated to your network, now don't forget to keep them in the loop with professional, consistent follow-up. Wherever appropriate, catch up with an e-mail, a phone call or a visit. Reconnect for networking success. Just be careful not to cross the line into obnoxious pushiness. Recognize the difference. Know when to pull back, but also know when to go forward.

Now that you know how to communicate better, let's see how you can *expand* your network for success.

"To my knowledge, the nirvana of networking consists of bringing the right people together at the right time to discuss the right subject and make the right decisions.

With Charles, I recognize the hunger in people to do business and the way he focuses that into the right direction. He does it his way, and shows real pleasure and lots of stamina in running a fast-growing international network and bringing people together."

- Emmanuel P. Gruijs, Director
AW - Europe

CHAPTER 4:

EXPANDING YOUR NETWORK

"Networking is a way of life. Make connections and build relationships everywhere you go."

- Charles Ruffolo, The NetworKing

Many people say to me, "You know everyone. How did you build your network so fast?"

Well, just like you and everyone else, I started with my family, friends, colleagues and clients, and others that already knew me. That was my core network. Then I took on the world.

If there's one thing that I want to impress upon you, it's that the world is *your* oyster when it comes to networking, the same as it's *my* oyster. Unless you hull that shell, however, you'll never realize the full potential of what's hidden.

Each and every one of you – no exceptions granted – have an unlimited network to build upon. It's infinite… but you must look past what's staring you in the face and activate the world beyond your familiar territory.

You've heard the expression "look outside the box." As cliché as it may be, that's precisely what you need to do to network your way to success. If you decide to stay in the box, you may as well close the lid.

Otherwise, lift the lid on your self-imposed limitations and learn how to *expand* your network for greater success.

The ground beneath your feet

To be blunt, your network is wherever your feet are – wherever there's another person in your vicinity. Waiting for a bus or train? Standing in an elevator with someone? Waiting in line at the supermarket? Don't day-dream – network! There's time for daydreaming later when you're sitting in your garden sipping a glass of wine that you got at a discount, I might add, because you networked.

Something as mundane as pumping gasoline at a service station can qualify for networking. I can prove it with a very simple example.

Once a week I leave my office and drive to a Shell gas station in town – the same one that I always "tank up" at on my way to Amsterdam. I stop there for several reasons, one of which is to collect the Shell stamps so that I can give them to my sister-in-law, Wendy, who saves them and appreciates me thinking of her. As it happens, I occasionally use the towels or other products at her house that she got by cashing in her stamps… my point being, what goes around comes around.

Another reason I go there is because I know the people who work there on a first-name basis, and they know me. Once I finish filling up the tank, I go inside to pay and am greeted either by Martijn, Albertine or Anneke, depending on who is working that day. I know all of their names because I've made it a point to do so. It doesn't take much effort when they're wearing nametags. You just need to pay attention to such things.

Invariably, I greet each one personally. When I first started doing this, they were shocked. You can imagine the look on their faces, wondering how I knew their names, then glancing down at their own nametags as if they had forgotten that they were wearing them.

Why do you think people wear nametags? They wear them so that the customers can address them properly, and as a way of showing friendliness and responsibility for their job. So I always utilize that tool to say their name out of respect.

As I've said before, people are never random. Anyone you may be tempted to regard as relatively insignificant just could be the vital link you need in your network for one or more of your current goals; likewise, there may be something they need that you can provide. Don't ignore anyone. Learn to pay attention *to everyone* around you.

I'm a regular at that Shell station and the attendants now know me well. If I ever, for example, lost or forgot my debit card or wallet, do you think that Martijn would tell me to siphon the gasoline back out, or that Albertine would say, "Leave your car here – there's a bus coming in five minutes…" or that Albertine would say, "Leave your car here – there's a bus coming in five minutes..." or that Anneke would say, "Sorry Charlie, but you cannot leave this gas station without paying…" ? Not likely. They are part of my network now. They know and trust me because I've built a rapport with them, and they will no doubt support me in time of need (as long as I don't abuse the privilege).

No, they're more likely to ask me to leave my business card and pay my debt the next time I come. I'm a regular customer and they know I'll be back. When a network is in place, you can rely on it.

Do you know someone well enough in your own network that you would receive credit if, for whatever reason, you could not pay for something at a certain moment? Do you have a regular place where you go that you could ask for something to be "put on your tab"?

I remember from my younger days when my parents had a tab at the local grocery store, and every time one of the Ruffolo kids would buy something on an errand to that store, we would put the charge on our tab. At the end of each month when my father got his paycheck, he would pay the shop owner, and everyone was happy. That's networking. Granted, it certainly didn't hurt that my brother Bobby worked there and the owner knew where he could get his money if necessary, but that simply meant that I had a further stake in the network that was already in place.

If you look for such opportunities, you'll be amazed at how you can expand your network to accomplish what you need or want to do.

Looking outside the box

In short, if you really want to expand your network, you must expand your horizons. Look around wherever you are. Tune in to your extended surroundings. Make no one exempt from your network. If you practice this, you'll be amazed at the results.

Regard everyone in your path as a potential source or beneficiary of your aims and goals. If you're stuck on class delineations, I can assure you right here and now that you'll have a problem networking. Unless you can get your nose out of the tree, you'll never be able to network.

Besides the person who happens to be standing next to you at this very moment, there are certain outlets that are conducive to expanding your network. First you've got to train yourself, however, to be Resourceful, with a capital "R". Resourceful people get ahead in whatever it is they want to accomplish. They leave a trail of dust behind on those who just don't know which way to turn, and who wallow their way through life.

Don't wait for networks to come to you. I repeat: Don't wait for networks to come to you. Find out, one way or another… and therein lies the key… where the people are that you need to reach. How?

1. Talk to everyone.
2. Search the Internet and use e-mail.

3. Join organizations and volunteer.
4. Socialize.
5. Sponsor your own event or party.

Let's take a look at each of these more closely.

Talk to everyone

I've already emphasized the value, in this chapter and the previous one, of carrying on a conversation with everyone you come across. Exclude no one, and find a link. I guarantee that this simple practice will lead to a wealth of connections important to your entire life.

When you do discover your links, do not be afraid or shy about asking for specific resources or favors. State clearly what you want or need. Don't beat around the bush; address your issue front and center.

Keep in mind, however, that some part of that conversation should also address what you can do for the other person. If you want people to be receptive to you, you must be always be receptive to their needs and wants. Conversation will illuminate what that may be if you gear it toward them.

Search the Internet and use e-mail

The Internet is a tool that you can't afford to ignore. Talk about connections! The Internet connects you to the entire world and back again. It's a godsend for many reasons, but of particular benefit to those who want to network. Simply plug in a reference to your particular need, passion or interest on any given search engine and, voila!…you've got the world on a string.

Internet searches can lead you in so many directions that a single mind can't even contemplate, let alone calculate, the possibilities. Tap into this powerful resource. Use the links presented within searches and convenient websites to hone in on resources for what you need.

Take notes on what you find in your searches, and contact the people pertaining to your goal. People who provide a website expect to be contacted, otherwise they wouldn't have one. Utilize websites to their fullest potential.

And while you're searching, keep in mind others in your network that may be looking for similar connections. Remember, the net swings both ways.

E-mail can also be used to maintain and expand your network. Always respond to legitimate e-mails. If someone in your network has taken the time to communicate with you via this, or any other format, take the time to respond.

Remember, one and one equals four. The other person's network is also your potential network. Foster the endless possibilities of that scenario by utilizing such rapid communications. Besides being common courtesy, responding to others' needs is also a clear way of giving back to your network. (More on that later.)

Join organizations and volunteer

Do you have any inkling of how many organizations are out there? How many do you belong to? Did you say "Zip"… as in zero?

If you did, set out to join one before the sun sets on your intentions. Organizations, clubs, interest groups… whatever you want to call them… are a vital resource for networking. Get some in your repertoire. Soon.

What kinds of organizations am I talking about? There are business clubs such as local Chambers of Commerce and special interest groups, such as societies for translators or editors, or professional societies such as the American Medical Association –virtually every endeavor has a pertinent club or association to which you can become a member if you belong to that genre. Whatever your particular profession, hobby or interest, there is bound to be a group somewhere out there that relates to it. And if there isn't, why not start one?

There are also numerous service and charitable organizations where you can make a big difference in someone else's life as well as your own by volunteering your time and talents. (More on this in Chapter 9.) Your own religious affiliation is one place to start. Beyond that, the "A" -"Z" of charities wishing for your involvement is staggering. Choose one, or more.

There are purely social clubs, some geared specifically to men or women, and some with a mix. Imagine whom you can meet at these.

In most countries, there is a dazzling array of publications covering the whole gamut of organizations. Visit your local library, bookshop or newsstand and do your homework to find out what's in your area. You'll be amazed at the prospects.

Essentially, you should never have a problem in finding activities, only a problem narrowing them down. If you train yourself to be resourceful, you'll have many more opportunities than time. It's the kind of "problem" we all need.

How else do you find these organizations? By asking around, contacting the local information office or Chamber of Commerce, perusing the Yellow Pages of the phonebook, and searching the Internet, as examples. Sharpen your resourcefulness skills and be proactive. If you don't go after that seat on the membership committee of the organization you're interested in, don't you think someone else will? And when they do, who do you think will be the first to reap the benefits of that network?

Many organizations have worldwide affiliations. Consider the ramifications of that! Again, the world is at your disposal. Grab it.

Granted, some organizations carry fairly high membership price tags. Others don't. Find your niche, consider your budget, and join a select few that meet your needs. Better yet, get invited as a guest to the ones you can't afford! Link up – by doing your homework – with someone who does belong to whichever group you wish to join. That way, at least for the first run, you can attend an initial meeting and make contacts. Who knows, perhaps you'll join one of their committees and get free membership in return.

As you can probably tell by now, I believe that where there's a will, there's a way. I certainly didn't invent that concept, but I do live and breathe it.

As you join and get involved in organizations for the value that they can bring to your network, keep in the forefront of your mind what you can give back. Sure, it takes time out of your busy days, but the payoffs for you and for those benefiting from your contributions are enormous. Volunteering is a great way to expand your network and give back.

Remember, "A" leads to "B", which leads to "C", and ad infinitum. One single person represents a network. Now think of the potential that a group of people represents. Whether it's the Boy or Girl Scouts that you've decided to help with or the local AIDS foundation, you can expand your network while greatly benefiting others.

Get out there and roll that networking snowball. By the end of your trail, your network should be so laden with contacts that you won't be able to lift it. Then and only then will you be able to say with confidence, "I'm networking."

Socialize

Although you can certainly socialize by joining organizations and the like, there are umpteen other ways to get out there and have a good time while networking. If you live anywhere where there are cultural activities at your disposal, imbibe. Go to museums, lectures, book readings, sports events, you name it, because, guess what? Other people go to these functions as well, and that means new contacts.

Allocate a certain amount of time in your life for some good solid socializing, and your network will grow –as long as you talk to the people at these venues, that is. If you go there but either clam up or stick only with your familiar buddies, you'll stay in your rut and never expand your network. As we discussed in Chapter 2 about building your network, sit by that stranger, not your friend or colleague. Idle on up to that unknown entity and introduce yourself.

And what do you do next? That's right, find a common link. You're definitely getting the hang of it.

As I've said, networking is simple … and fun. If you stay at home in couch-potato mode, however, your network will only reach from your remote control to the device at the other end. If you make an effort to socialize, your network – and I daresay your general quality of life —will improve.

Find out where a crowd gathers, and go.

Sponsor your own event or party

If going out to events is truly a challenge for you, for whatever reason, why not sponsor your own event or gathering in the comfort of your home or preferred location? In other words, invite people – not only your best friends, but their friends as well, to your party or event..

Everyone loves a party or invitation to something. Use your imagination. The challenge with this, however, is to invite those that you don't know very well, and then to devote a large part of your time talking to them rather than only to your friends. When was the last time you held a party? Perhaps it's time.

Likewise, when you're invited to a party, make a conscious effort to meet new people that will add to your network. And remember to follow-up with the new relationships by calling, e-mailing or visiting them when appropriate. Otherwise, what's the point of fostering new relationships?

Stretch your horizons

In the end, you've got to choose what works best for you to expand your network. Consider expanding the circles where you normally operate, and then direct your efforts as far outside the box as you possibly can.

As Wouter van Rhoon, Team Leader for MCI in The Netherlands, recently said at one of my seminars, "A network can never be extensive enough – and you can never utilize it enough. I realized that I was only using about 1% of my potential network, when I could have been using 100%."

How much are you using?

Perhaps you need to *energize*. Let's learn how to feed the fire.

"Everybody knows that if you want to be successful you have to go out and talk. Talk with as many people as possible. Most people only talk with other people if they presume that there is a direct benefit for their business. It is better to talk with EVERYBODY you meet – especially with those who you would not expect to be of any help. That is the principal idea of networking.

More often than not, those people will come up with something interesting that can make your business – or someone else's business – more successful. Don't be afraid... just do it!

Charles Ruffolo discovers networking opportunities in every single contact he makes. He is brilliant in connecting people. Every contact he makes will come back to him with something interesting in the future. He knows this system as no one else, and he believes in it."

-Max van Rijswijk, General Manager
Natural Synergy
The Netherlands

Origins of the Ruffolo network – Ruf's grandfather, Frank, (standing, back) and his grandmother, Amelia (Sorrentino), holding his father, baby Joseph Patrick, as they arrived from Cerisano (Cosenza), Italy.

Ruffolo and his mother, Clara E. Welsh, in America (L), and Ruf's wife, Herma, and her mother, Anneke Broesder-Hoogland, in The Netherlands, not knowing that their networks would merge..

Ruffolo's parents, Joseph en Clara, at a U.S. Steel company picnic at Kennywood Park near Pittsburgh, Pennsylvania.

"Ruf" at a very young networking age in Pittsburgh.

Ruffolo's father, Joseph P. Ruffolo (L), and his father-in-law, Jan A. Broesder – his favorite mentors and friends networking in The Netherlands.

General Wilson, U.S. Army, shaking hands with Ruffolo as he goes from being dressed in uniform to dressed for success..

George Foreman signing a wooden figure of his own image that Ruffolo made in high school some 30 years earlier – the "common ground" that Ruf used as a conversation piece with the heavyweight boxing champion..

Herma and Charles Ruffolo with the 42nd President of the United States, The Honorable William Jefferson Clinton, during his visit that Ruffolo arranged to The Netherlands

Ruffolo with his father-in-law, Jan A. Broesder (L), his wife Herma, President Clinton, and sisters-in-law, Anneke de Vente-Broesder, and Louise van Setten-Broesder, in a family photo requested by the President.

Students, representing five years of the Giving Back Foundation, who volunteered to help during President Clinton's visit. Pictured, at the President's request, are (L to R) Dutch politician Fatima Elatik, Sana Ali (2000), Tejuna Veldhuizen (1999), Dutch celebrity Jimmy Geduld (back), President Clinton, Fadoua Ibn Said (2001), Nur Icar (back) (2003), Dwayne Gefferie (2002), and Ruffolo..

Tom Houck (R), former chauffeur of Dr. Martin Luther King, Jr., giving Ruffolo the "Giving Back handshake" during a visit to The Netherlands in support of the Giving Back Foundation.

Ruf, The NetworKing, working the floor at his Network Club Winter Event in Amsterdam, The Netherlands.

Members and guests at The Network Club Autumn Event at De Kentering in Rosmalen, The Netherlands.

Ruffolo leading the crowd at his Network Club Summer Event at De Westerbouwing in Oosterbeek (Arnhem), The Netherlands.

Ruffolo giving prize tickets to the children of Kevin Sparkman, Director of Kevin's Party Service, during The Network Club Family Day at Six Flags Holland in Biddinghuizen..

The NetworKing (R) in action during The Network Club European Event in Maastricht, The Netherlands.

NFL Commissioner Paul Tagliabue (L) with Buford Alexander (R) and Ruffolo in support of the NFL teams and the Giving Back Foundation during the NFL European Leagues World Bowl game held in Amsterdam.

CHAPTER 5:

ENERGIZING YOUR NETWORK

"The ability to energize your network is what makes all the difference."

- Charles Ruffolo, The NetworKing

O.K., you've figured out *where* you're going to network – everywhere. Now, how do you get your network to work for you? What does it take to get it fired up and shifted into high gear?

You can talk until you're blue in the face about all the contacts you've made through your networking, but if you don't energize that network, it will be like cement – plastered, but merely holding up the wall between you and countless connections that could make a real difference in your life.

Hopefully by now you're making a concerted effort to talk to strangers, communicating as effectively as you can, and expanding your network by being everywhere humanly possible.

The next issue is how to set the crucial task of networking into action. That is how do you *energize* your network for success?

Of might and means

I can relate two true stories to you that illustrate, without unnecessary theorizing, how to energize your network. The first involves a mighty acquisition... the second, an even mightier political figure. As with any effective networking scheme, both involved careful planning and connections, and prove that you can achieve virtually anything in life if you energize your network. Anything.

These stories are also examples of creating your own opportunities. So often I hear people talking about being "lucky" or "in the right place at the right time". As I've said, I do not believe in luck. I contend that people to whom good things happen usually have set themselves up to succeed. Even if you are in the right place at the right time but either through ignorance, laziness, shyness or fear, you don't make things happen, no amount of luck, in my mind, will bridge the gap.

You, and only you, are the catalyst that can energize your network.

You want what?

As you may have guessed by now, the word "impossible" is a non-entity in my vocabulary. The concept just doesn't exist for me. Perhaps it doesn't exist for you either.

Regardless, it's a fair guess to say that probably everyone has had some goal in life that he or she initially thought was impossible but, in the end, achieved it. What do you think was most likely the key reason for that success? Exactly – energy – the determination, power and will to activate the process to reach your goal. In short, energizing your network for success.

Such was the case when an advertising agency in Amsterdam called me because they had heard that I was a Professional Networker and that I was good at what I did.

"Yes, I'm a Professional Networker," I replied, "and yes, I must be good if you've called me. How can I help you?"

"Well, we need an aircraft carrier, Charles, for a mega-promotion for two of our multi-national clients here in The Netherlands. The idea is to hold a Millennium Celebration party off the coast of Barcelona to increase brand awareness and preference among a key target group of 18-25-year-olds in the European market. Participants will be selected on the basis of their sales promotion activities."

"You realize, of course, that an aircraft carrier is a war machine? Who are these clients?"

"That's confidential at the moment, Charles. Can you help?"

In my inimitable style, my brain immediately segued to how I, Charles Douglas Armando Ruffolo, could in heaven's name acquire an aircraft carrier. Needless to say, it wasn't something I had in my back pocket. However, because it's difficult for me to ever say "no", I firmly believed that there was someone in my network that I could count on to deliver. Armed with my adopted philosophy that "where there's a will there's a way", I was determined to find their party vessel.

"An aircraft carrier, huh?" I said, sitting straight up at the sheer prospect.

"Yeh," those of little faith replied with a smirk. "Think you can do it or not?"

My brain isn't known for its quick synapses for nothing. Even before the molecules could align themselves, I was taking on the challenge.

"No problem. Give me a few days." And I hung up the phone.

How on earth, I reeled, was I going to find an aircraft carrier, let alone

one that could be bought or rented? Was I nuts? Not at all – just pleasantly challenged. Quite frankly though, I couldn't believe that someone wanted to use a war machine, no less, for a sales promotion!

Military man that I was, however, I knew first-hand what an aircraft carrier could do, and the attention that one would bring to such an event. In short, I knew I was hooked. By energizing my network, I would pull it off.

I looked out over the picturesque canal in Giethoorn near my home and thought, "Nope. Too shallow…. but hold on. That canal goes out to a bigger canal that eventually ends up in Rotterdam, the largest port in the world. One thing leads to another, does it not? Somehow I'll make the connection."

With that, I embarked on what to most would seem like mission impossible. With determination and energy, I would, indeed, find an aircraft carrier just waiting in the wings to be outfitted for a sales blitz bar none. My 20 years in the military weren't for naught, I thought as I gathered my composure. Surely I could energize those connections and find a stockpiled aircraft carrier ... somewhere.

The question was: Where would I begin to energize my network with this goal in mind? Did I think it would be "a piece of cake"? No. A good challenge? You bet!…about as big of a challenge as I could ever expect … and I relished the mere thought.

USS CABOT (CVL 28)

Thirty-six hours later, I had an aircraft carrier.

Talk about energizing! I went into overdrive. By figuring out in Mach-force time who I knew and who they knew in turn, my key figures were materialized. It was clear that I needed to energize my military and government network…fast.

First thing I did was to call Angelo Borelli, for whom I had worked in a U.S. government office in The Netherlands.

“Hey, Paisano… yeah, the business world is crazy but great… The thing is, Ange, I need an aircraft carrier. Where can I get one?”

“Ruffolo,” he laughed, “you never cease to amaze me.”

“Well, it’s not for me,” and I told him the story.

Before I knew it, I had a contact name in Rotterdam. I called him on Angelo’s referral, and this person in turn referred me to someone in the United States.

By contacting that third person, I found out that the USS Cabot/SNS Dedalo, also known as “The Iron Lady” – one of the most decorated ships of World War II – was about to be dismantled. Maybe I could save it through this project. The ship, after all, had high historic value and a legendary reputation, having participated in nearly every major campaign in the Pacific, surviving two separate kamikaze attacks, and never needing to go into port for repairs. What a showcase that would be!

Next thing I knew I was talking to the organization that owned the aircraft carrier, and explaining my mission… complete with details about a floating disco with live entertainment, the likes of which Tina Turner and the Rolling Stones might be featured, with world-class catering and a slew of other activities taking place on the various decks.

The ship in question was docked in Brownsville, Texas, and would have to be towed to the port of Barcelona off the coast of Spain. “What would it take,” I asked, “to get it off the market and into my possession?”

Their answer was that I would need to place an option to purchase the aircraft carrier. Because of the magnitude of such a purchase, I first, wisely, checked with my wife Herma. Then I purchased, for several thousand dollars, an option for none other than an aircraft carrier, knowing that the agency and their clients would have to purchase it from me.

“We need to talk,” I said to the agency. “I have the aircraft carrier, but I need to know who the clients are before we proceed any further.”

They gave me the names of two Dutch multi-national companies, both of whose directors I happened to know! My network and my mission were complete.

To this day, people continue to be amazed that I managed to find, purely by energizing my extensive network, the only aircraft carrier available on the international market. Talk about a rush. For me it was the epitome of networking.

Moral of this story? - *nothing* is impossible if you build a network and energize it. But success only happens when planning and preparation meet opportunity. That chemical reaction involves pure energy on your part.

Did the most celebrated party take place on that aircraft carrier? Unfortunately not. The waters of the world got a little murky at that time, so it was shelved due to security concerns, and my option to buy the carrier was dropped. And yes, I got all my out of pocket costs back... Did I accomplish my goal? Absolutely. My network came through, loud and clear.

Yours can too, if you energize it.

Mr. President, Charles Ruffolo here ...

Unless you live in the United Kingdom where you dare not speak to the Queen without formal permission and an approved dialogue, or some other country where a similar protocol dictates, I figure that everyone is fair game.

Such was the case in 2002 when I was presented with the challenge of getting former United States President Clinton to come to The Netherlands on behalf of a Dutch corporation's effort to connect business people with the American market. President Clinton would be the guest of honor, and the obvious draw to the proposed event, but where would I start? How would I energize my network?

Well, I knew that President Clinton and I had one very clear things in common: we were both American citizens and we had a military connection – he *was*, after all, my Commander in Chief. By virtue of that fact, I quickly deduced that I could begin by energizing the vast network at work for me in the United States – my government.

The first question that came to my mind was, "Whom did I know that personally knew the former President?" Well, as an expatriate on Dutch soil, I had made the acquaintance of the then Ambassador to The Netherlands, the Honorable K. Terry Dornbush, whom I knew to be a very approachable man. I would start there. Throughout the years, Ambassador Dornbush has been a good friend to me, both during and after his time in office in The Netherlands, where he decided to reside. So I called him in Atlanta, Georgia, where he happened to be at that moment.

"Sir, Ruf here. Ambassador, I need to arrange for former President Clinton to come to The Netherlands as the guest of honor at a business function hosted by a client of mine. How do I get through to his office, sir? Can you help me?"

The wheels began turning and the necessary links formed in a matter of seconds.

"If necessary, Ambassador," I continued, "we'll fly you to President Clinton's office to clinch the deal. This event has to go on."

"No, that's not necessary," he assured me.

He then advised me how to contact the appropriate person and also suggested that I let his successor, Ambassador Cynthia P. Schneider, know what I was trying to do.

"Will do." And I did.

The former Ambassador Schneider was cycling in North Carolina when I connected, and I asked her if she could help me arrange to bring former President Clinton to The Netherlands, and proceeded to explain the mission. In turn, she confirmed the appropriate contact that Ambassador Dornbush had provided. I immediately called the scheduling office for President Clinton and began arranging the visit.

Within three weeks, we had a signed contract. Thanks to the power of networking and my personal connections, I was able to arrange for a former United States President to come to The Netherlands.

Over the next few months, I worked intensely with numerous agents and offices of the President, particularly his Advance Teams who thoroughly checked out the venue where he is scheduled to go. I had the honor and privilege of working closely with them, including spending some treasured downtime playing cards.

Never in my wildest dreams did I ever think that I would be playing host to a U.S. President and ultimately sitting with my family and close friends at the head table with him.

But sure enough, on the 15th of December, 2002, The Honorable William Jefferson Clinton, 42nd President of the Unites States, came to The Netherlands due to my networking efforts.

What made this possible? Well, it all comes down to whom you know and, more importantly, who knows *you*, coupled with much determination and hard work, plus a strong sense of faith, trust and respect for the system and the players. I had energized my network, and the awesome power of networking had proven itself once again.

Pictures speak louder than words, so take a look at the photo gallery in the center of this book where there is a photo of President Clinton together with my wife and me that day. You can bet that it was worth the hassle and the effort when our former Commander in Chief shook my hand and, to my total surprise, said to the audience during his speech, "I want to give a special thanks to my dear friend, Charles Ruffolo, who made it possible for me to come to Holland."

Success. The client was happy, and I was thrilled to have been able to make it all happen. By energizing my broad network and building a rapport with the former President's office, it all come together.

In the heat of battle, your network does not abandon you – and vice versa. If I say that something will happen, it happens. That's because I know how to energize my network.

Obviously, you can do the same. After all, if a wayward boy from Pittsburgh can get through to a United States President, or anyone else for that matter, so can you.

On the runway at Rotterdam airport, President Clinton asked me if I'd like to fly back to New York with him. Unfortunately, I had to turn him down because, believe it or not, I had other commitments to keep that involved quality time with my wife and family. Maybe next time, Mr. President.

Feed the fire

No one has a more powerful network than you; you just need to energize it. See what you have in your personal toolbox and use it. Be innovative; and direct your efforts straight toward your goal.

Figure out who in your network can help you to accomplish the things you need or want to accomplish. And then energize by contacting those who can make a difference in your life, or you in theirs.

As another former U.S. President, John F. Kennedy, once said, "There are risks and costs to action, but they are far less than the long-range risks of comfortable inaction."

Once you do get into the habit of energizing your network, you'll see how easy it is to keep the momentum going. You'll have so many good things flowing your way – *and* toward others – that you'll find it hard to keep up with the backlog.

If you *really* want to feed the fire and give your friends, colleagues, customers, shareholders or business relations something to cheer about, energize your network even further by giving back to them. Then you've energized full circle.

In the process, remember that energizing your network should involve putting your best self forward. That brings us directly to our next issue: *leading* your network for success.

"As one gets older and more experienced, the resume, textbooks and other "on paper" qualifications become increasingly less meaningful. However strong the realization of the power of contacts becomes, few people do more than go through the motions of collecting business cards, making some phone calls and joining a club.

...Ruffolo, on the other hand, truly believes in people and understands the power of collective energy."

- Steven van Tongeren, CPA
United States

CHAPTER 6:

LEADING YOUR NETWORK

"You can influence others by talking about what they want and showing them how to get it. That's leadership."

- Charles Ruffolo, The NetworKing

If you sit at the back of a theatre, the cast won't see you. Those in the forefront of networks know how to be seen and respected by the cast of characters needed to network their way to success. They lead, and their network follows.

Even if you consider yourself more of a follower than a leader, there are some basic management skills you can apply to enhance your leadership posture in your network.

As with most things in life, there's a human dimension to networking. How you succeed at networking depends to a great deal on how you lead. By focusing on the human dimension of networking, you can learn to lead your network where you want it to go. By applying your own personal attributes toward inspiring others, you can *lead* your network to success.

Lead and they will follow

Leading your network with conviction is paramount to networking your way to success. Without a lengthy business school lecture, I'll share some of the foundations upon which you can build your own brand of leadership. Everyone's style is different, of course, but if you develop your own flair for leadership, you'll be sitting front and center all your life.

Let's start with a simple visualization task.

Identifying a good leader

Who do you truly respect as a leader in your life? Visualize someone. Is it an athletic coach, your boss, a professor, the leader of your country, the president of an organization, or your mother or father, husband, wife or partner?

Now think about what that person does that made him or her such a *good* leader in your eyes. Here are a few examples:

- Handles conflict well
- Communicates well
- Organizes or plans well
- Gives consistent directions
- Treats employees or others with respect
- Responds to requests with enthusiasm and conviction
- Never puts anyone down in public
- Motivates others
- Tunes into and turns onto life in all respects
- "Knows their stuff", i.e. their job or skill
- Delegates
- Makes quick but effective decisions
- Has a strong sense of humor
- Promotes fairness
- Uses their intelligence constructively

Now think about someone you know who's been a very *poor* leader. Unfortunately, we often know more people in this category than the first, or at least we can instantly conjure up more examples of such. Take all the attributes above and turn them into negatives.

Which category do you fit in: good or poor leader? A little of both? Probably.

How, then, can you develop more of the attributes of a good leader and go on to lead your network?

My "The NetworKing 8C Leadership Principle" is a good place to start:

Characteristics of Leadership Principle

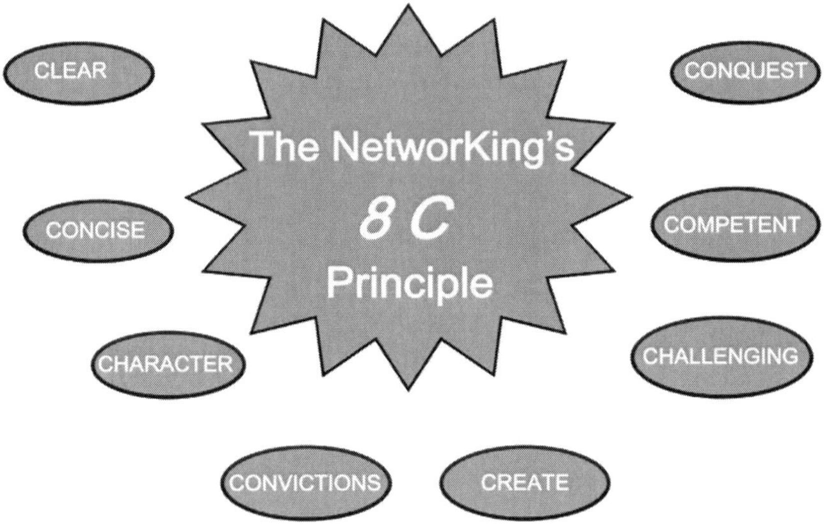

Clear, Concise, Character, and Convictions Create Challenging Competent Conquest

Let's translate the above illustration into specifics, based on some of the skills you've already learned in the preceding chapters.

Principles of leading your network:

1. *Know your network*. You can't energize and lead a network if you don't know whom it is that you need to lead.
2. *Build trust*. Are you reliable? Why or why not? Work at becoming more reliable. Keep your convictions and promises, or don't make them.
3. *Display ethical standards*. You know what's right from wrong, so live by it.
4. *Demonstrate character.* Your character will demonstrate your true colors. Make sure it's a rainbow.
5. *Prepare for the worst.* Things do not always work out as we would like. Have a back-up plan and remember, we're dealt the cards of life and have to play them.
6. *Take your network with you.* Too many people forget to bring their

network with them as they explore other networks. Name-drop where appropriate.

7. *Combine and share your network.* There are more contacts out there to go around than you may think. By combining your network with others, you expand and feed both. There are a lot of opportunities that you can't readily see, but others in your network may recognize them for you. Same thing works in reverse. Identify networks on the other side of the fence.
8. *Connect with your network.* This means doing things with the people in your network, socially and/or professionally, and making an effort to understand their needs and wants.
9. *Lead your network.* Provide purpose, direction and motivation by bringing together everything that you know how to do.
10. *Give to your network.* This is the cardinal rule of networking. The challenge is to give without a hidden agenda. Remember, all things work for the best.

Basic leadership principles

Leadership is the art of using direct or indirect power to influence the thoughts and actions of others in such a way that they succeed in achieving high performance and desired results.

Leaders are not born; they are made. You don't inherit leadership the same way as you do hair or eye color. It's a skill that can be learned and perfected with practice.

The first premise is to realize that every person and organization is different, so leadership modes will be different, depending on your particular situation. The environment in which you lead is shaped by everything that goes on around you, by who you are and what you know, as well as by the participants and what *they* know.

In order to lead your network, you must interact and energize with respect, integrity, honor and reliability. These precepts are crucial. Only then will you be able to inspire others through purpose, motivation, support, vision and direction, with the result of accomplishing a certain task.

Leading your network is the result of:

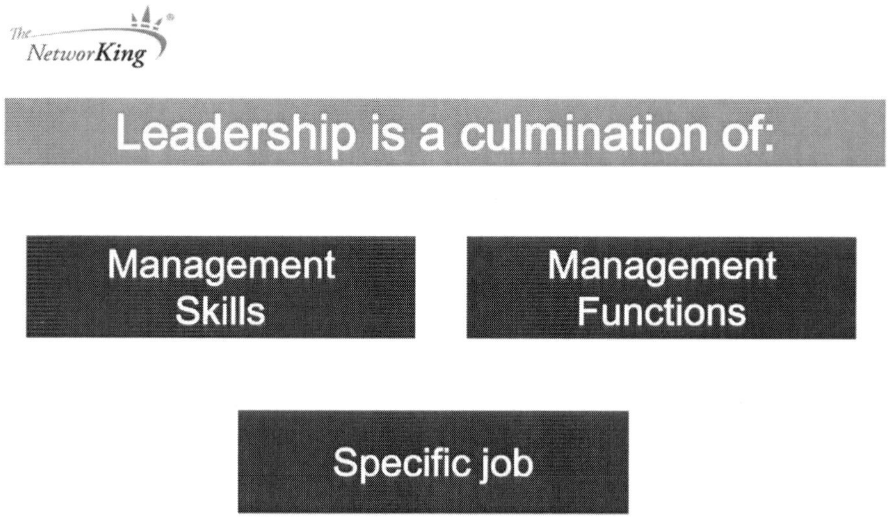

Business management is objective and measurable – you want to get from point "A" to point "B", and your performance can be measured. Leadership, on the other hand, is purely subjective. It's virtually impossible to measure.

As a leader, you have been entrusted with responsibility. How you prepare yourself for that role, and how you learn and embrace the values inherent in that role, determine your success as a leader.

The ability to lead is acquired through the experiences of everyday life. It requires constant study, hard work and frequent practice. Because you are dealing with people and their emotions, dreams and fears, it also calls for a strong dose of imagination and a positive, upbeat attitude.

Let's lock now all my "ABC of Leadership".

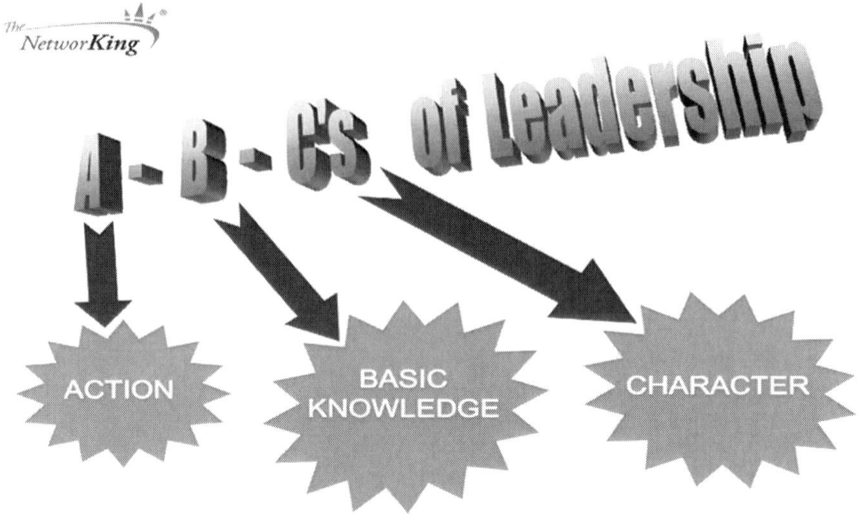

Action

Leadership is demonstrated through your behavior. Behavior is based on your own personal values, attributes and character – your inner strengths. Ultimately, actions always speak louder than words.

Your ability to lead others is directly influenced by your attitude. Your attitude and, subsequently, your actions set the tone for your leadership. Day to day, task to task, minute to minute, you communicate your attitude through your actions.

Optimism spiced with a strong sense of humor goes a long way toward building a respected leader. No one likes a pessimist, a sourpuss or a tyrant.

Your actions determine your leadership style and influence your entire network.

Basic knowledge

In order to be regarded as competent, a leader must proffer a certain level of knowledge and skill – basic professional knowledge on the one hand, and people skills on the other. Focus on and develop your personal bank of knowledge and skills necessary for the tasks at hand.

Character

Your attitudes about the worth of people make up your values and, therefore, your character.

Realize that the people in your network also come with a character formed by background, experience, education, religion and philosophical beliefs and, ultimately, their own set of values – an intricate, lifelong conglomeration.

Let's emphasize certain things about values:

- Values are more than a system of rules. They're a person's core approach to life.
- People come with their own set of values.
- People are shaped by values.
- Values remind you to value people. Treat people with dignity and respect, and do not violate the values of others. Respect their differences.
- Incorporate values into your own actions.
- Teach others to accept and live by values.

Likewise, people are shaped and driven by emotions. You influence others by talking about what they want and showing them how to get it. But the best way to lead someone to do something is to make that person *want* to do it. Coercion is never good leadership. Support and effective communications work better.

Types of power

An important facet of leadership is making the most of opportunities that you have, and using other means to exert influence when possible.

We all have multiple types of power at our disposal: legitimate power, such as that of a mother or father or a supervisor; reward power, such as promotions or awards; coercive power, such as the power of persuasion or even threats; and the four powers that are most important to networking: *reference power, expert power, information power and willpower*. Let's concentrate on those that relate most to networking.

Reference power is true networking in action. By providing and seeking references –personal and professional contacts – you direct your destiny and the destinies of others. I demonstrated this very clearly with my actions to get President Clinton to come to The Netherlands. The power of my references played a key role in getting his scheduling officers to listen to me, and in securing the visit.

Expert power is sharing your expertise and, likewise, tapping into the expertise of others. Everyone has strengths and skills. Determine what yours are and utilize them to get you where you want to go, and to help others.

For example, I've based my life around networking. As a result, I'm regarded as an expert on the subject, and have taken on the designation of The NetworKing (cleverly conceptualized by Stephanie Ward of Firefly Coaching in The Netherlands, www.FireflyCoaching.com). Turning networking into a pure and practical science – by giving my HAND Networking Program, by providing the impetus for networking opportunities via my website www. TheNetworKing.com and by speaking to groups and writing this book about networking – has given me the power to be a networking expert. People in my network now recognize me as the The NetworKing. That's expert power.

Information power is sharing your basic knowledge with those who can benefit from it and, in return, growing and learning from the vast pool of untapped knowledge at your fingertips.

Information power levels the playing field. The more information you have, the more prepared and confident you will be, whether it involves your business, a purchase or the test you have to take tomorrow. When you "know who is coming to dinner and what's on the menu", so to speak, you can use that information power to build, communicate to, energize, expand, and lead your network.

Willpower is the chemistry of success that energizes your hidden potential to lead. Motivation, self-reliance and determination make up willpower. They give you the courage and the impetus to get things moving and shaking in your life. By relying on your own resources – your network – and your abilities, by setting goals and exercising the actions to achieve those goals, you are using your willpower to lead your network. You may have all the references, expertise and information at your disposal, but if you don't have the willpower to use them, you'll get nowhere.

The end goal

When you can act and bring together everything within your power to provide purpose, direction and motivation in the lives of those with whom you come in contact, you'll be ready to lead your network. It's all about bringing the best and the most out of you and others.

Leaders set the culture for organizations and make the difference between mediocre and exceptional performance. The ultimate "ABC's" of leading your network consist of *action*, the behavior put forth to accomplish a given task, based on what your character tells you is right for the situation; *basic knowledge*, the information and skills required to get the job done properly; and having *character*, that combination of values and attributes that underlie your ability to get things done and influence others to follow you. Combined, that's leadership. Once you've applied the attributes of a leader, your next step is to pump up your network with *motivation* and *enthusiasm*.

"It is – or should be – common knowledge that if you make someone feel good, that person will behave as a good person and act in accordance with his feeling. As a result, he will be – or has a better chance to be – successful.

... If people are around "Ruf", they want to please (i) him and (ii) the people around him. The beautiful thing is that, even when he leaves, the 'good spirit' stays."

- Godfried Kinnegim, Lawyer, Allen & Overy
The Netherlands

CHAPTER 7:

MOTIVATING & ENTHUSING YOUR NETWORK

"No one was ever a success who wasn't first motivated and enthused."

- Charles Ruffolo, The NetworKing

Do you often wonder why some people appear to be highly motivated and enthused while others do not? If you have teenagers, you may have wondered this quite often.

Well, the good news, Mom and Dad, is that motivation and enthusiasm are not personal traits – that is, something that some people have and others do not. If an employer, or a parent, labels a person as lazy, for example, such a label assumes that that person is always lazy. This is simply not true.

Be honest. Are you ever lazy? Aren't there times when you'd just rather not do something simply because you just don't feel like it or can't be bothered? Sure there are. We're all lazy at times.

The same thing holds true for motivation and enthusiasm. In general, the situation at hand determines whether or not we're motivated or enthused. Going to the dentist or doctor is, for example, is not very motivating and, as a whole, we don't get very enthusiastic about it. However, give a sports fan such as myself the opportunity to attend a Pittsburgh Steeler's football game, for example, and I'll show you true motivation and enthusiasm. Give another person the chance to hear his or her favorite singer in concert, and they too will be motivated and enthused.

We all get motivated and enthused about certain things in our lives – even teenagers. Granted, they may not get motivated and enthused about the same things that you do, but they do get motivated by their own agendas and interests. In the military, we were motivated and enthused to get home alive. Sports figures are motivated and enthused to win.

What lights your fire? What gets you motivated and enthused? And how can you make it happen more often?

If motivation and enthusiasm are not traits but situational characteristics, doesn't it follow that we can set ourselves up, or discipline ourselves, to be more motivated and enthused when the situation calls for it? Sure it does. *Motivation* and *enthusiasm* can be learned.

Follow ME.

Webster and "ME"

Motivation and enthusiasm, which I refer to as "ME", constitute the core of your potential networking success. Without it, your network won't get off the ground.

You can know your network, communicate to your network, energize your network, and lead your network, but if you don't exhibit motivation and enthusiasm for your network, it will droop and drop dead in its tracks. Motivation and enthusiasm, combined, is the "push that comes to shove" when something needs to get done.

Webster's dictionary defines motivation as "an incentive or motive", and enthusiasm as "an intense feeling for a subject or cause." The combination of the two is dynamite – in fact, it's the essential power you need to carry your network to the next level.

All theories aside

If there were ever a theory for anything, motivation might well win hands down for the number formulated. For hundreds of years, the question of motivation has been bombarded with fancy-sounding theories with names like the Hierarchy of Needs Theory, the Goal-setting Theory, the Three Needs Theory, the ERG Theory, the Cognitive Evaluation Theory, the Reinforcement Theory, the Equity Theory, the Expectancy Theory, the Motivation Hygiene Theory, and even the Theory X and Theory Y theories – all legitimate in their individual approaches. These theories primarily addressed the fact that if employees can be motivated to produce just slightly more than their usual output, the economic rewards to individual organizations and, indeed, society as a whole would be immense. The focus is on employees and productivity; I transfer motivational theories to everyday life.

What all these motivation theories boil down to is that if we manage our mind energy, we will generate mental endurance and, therefore, success – both personal and professional. In terms of networking, motivation means the difference between connecting for success or not. It's that critical of an element.

Simpley stated, motivation is an inner desire to reach a higher level of wellbeing. If the rewards are important enough, we usually get motivated enough to pursue them. Hence, if you really want to network for success, you first must get motivated to do so.

Enthusiasm plays a key role in achieving motivation. In fact, they feed upon each other. You can want something badly enough, i.e. to be motivated, but not have enough enthusiasm to generate a positive outcome. As Ralph Waldo Emerson said, "Nothing great was ever achieved without enthusiasm."

The word "enthusiasm" is a fascinating word in itself. It comes from the Greek word, "enthousiasmos", deriving from the adjective "entheos", or "having the God within." Literally, it is formed from two words: "en", meaning "in or within", and "Theos", meaning "God or divine power." So enthusiasm literally means "expressing the God within, or to be inspired by a God." No matter how you look at it, it's a powerful word.

People often say to me, "Ruf, you are just too motivated and enthused." To that I respond: How can one be too motivated or enthused? Excitement breeds enthusiasm, as in a game of sport where the players are motivated and enthused to go the extra mile. Why do you think we have "Employee of the Month" or "Student of the Year"? - to motivate and enthuse and get the momentum going to breed success. In my opinion, you can never have enough of those elements.

Having said that, it is possible to express a lot of enthusiasm about something, but just not be motivated enough to go for it. The two concepts work neck and neck.

With that in mind, I formulated my own theory. It's not a complicated or esoteric one. I just call it "ME", an acronym for motivation and enthusiasm, because the momentum starts within ME… or you, as the case may be. You've got to light your own fire to be successful at networking. Motivation and enthusiasm are the kindling and the matches needed.

The NetworKing "ME" Theory

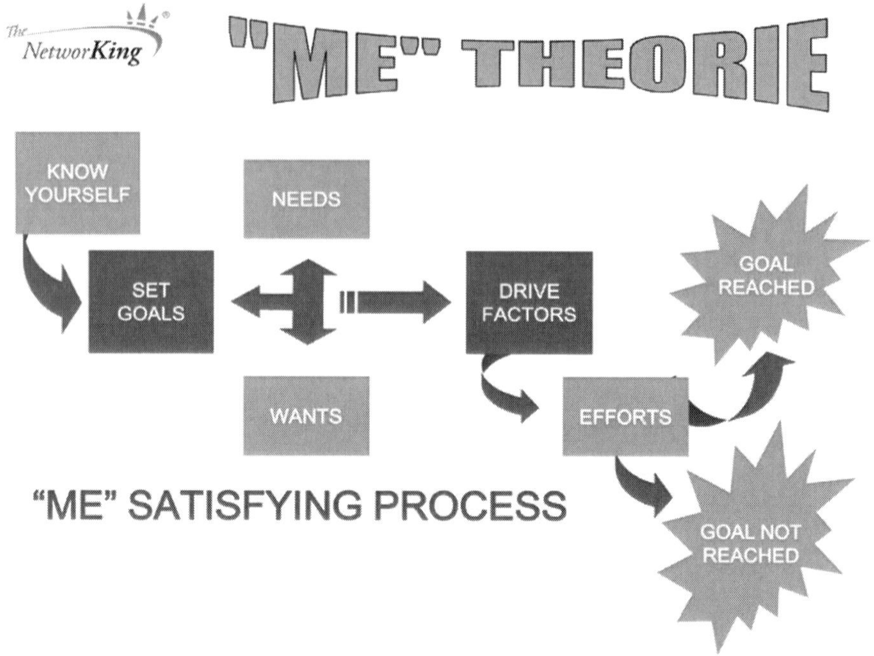

Key elements in my RIBS "ME" Theory for networkers are:

- *Know yourself.*

Look at others around you and then look at yourself. Be honest. What are you good and not good at? Take time to watch others, to study good role models and learn how to turn your weaknesses into strengths. If it means taking a course in interpersonal skills or public speaking, realize the benefits of doing so and go out and do it.

If you really want to know about yourself, ask others who know you and see you daily. Then deal with the truth. Do you have integrity, i.e. do you tell the truth to both yourself and others? Are you loyal, i.e. do you discuss issues only with those who have a need to know? Do you have endurance, i.e. maintaining the physical and mental stamina to do what is necessary? Are you dependable, i.e. can you be counted on to do the things you're asked to do or that you promise to do, in a complete and timely manner? Are you decisive, i.e. do you study your alternatives and carefully select the best course of action within a reasonable amount of time? Do you use good judgement, i.e. do you consider all possible effects of what you're about to do before you do it? Do you take initiative, i.e. do you take action in a situation where something must be done, even in the absence of direction from someone else? And finally, do you have a sense of humor, i.e. are you able to have fun doing what you do and keep a light perspective on life?

Successful people succeed because they know themselves better than anyone else.

- *Set goals.*

Do you want to increase market share or find a better-paying job? Set goals that will point you in the right direction. Goal setting helps you to determine when you've arrived, or if you've gotten off track. Without concrete goals, chance and circumstance will determine where you'll go.

Successful people succeed because they know where they want to go.

- *Determine your needs and wants.*

You can't have reasonable goals until you determine your needs and wants. Distinguish the two, and go for those most dear to your heart or necessary. Identify what's important to you. Ask yourself, what do I need in my life, or what would I like to have or achieve in my life? Your mindset determines the outcome of your goals.

Successful people succeed because they know their needs and wants.

- *Decide what drives or motivates you.*

Drive factors generate a positive mental attitude that helps you find ways to reach your particular goals. Ask yourself, "What motivates me? What drives me to succeed?" Your drive factors represent your desire and commitment toward reaching your goals.

Successful people succeed because they know what drives or motivates them.

- *Make the effort.*

Goals are achieved through effort. Nobody is going to carry the ball for you. Either stick your neck out or go back in the hole. Which do you choose?

Results stem from your direct interaction in a situation that causes you to reach – or not reach – your goal. If you *don't* reach your goal, be ready to calculate the loss and quickly address the future with determination and a revised plan.

Successful people succeed because they make the effort to succeed.

Remember, to win you need to play. And to play you need to know and follow the rules of the game.

Let's look at more specific guidelines for motivating and enthusing yourself and your network.

How to motivate yourself

Sometimes it's harder to motivate yourself than it is to motivate others. Once you've chosen your goal and a course of action that targets the best-perceived outcome, how do you motivate yourself to carry it through?

Motivation is the underlying basis for what you think and do. It's simply the set of needs and wants that you have, given an injection of willpower. As I've said, it can be learned.

Here's how:

- *Reflect on your successes.* No one can inspire you as much as yourself. Sit back and reflect on the successes in your life – like getting your high-school diploma or university degree, or starting your own company. For me, success is having served 20 years in the U.S. military and having my own networking business. Determine what success has meant for you.

- *Establish a support channel for yourself.* Your support channel consists of the people with whom you can talk about what matters most in your life. My support channel begins with my wife Herma and extends to my family and broad network of supporters. If I fall, which I often do, they are there to help me. Who is in your support channel?
- *Dream and visualize your actions.* Sports figures are always dreaming about winning the championship. Do the same thing in your life. Dream about the family you plan to have, the vacation you wish to take, or the business you hope to start. Be prepared at the same time, however, to know what you will do next if that dream is not realized. Visualize opposing scenarios, but do dream.
- *Set the example in things that you do.* Like it or not, people in your network are watching you. The power of example is enormous. Set an example by maintaining high but attainable goals and standards, and ensuring that your actions match.
- *Reward yourself when you have earned it.* When you reach a goal, reward yourself, whether it simply means going to a movie, taking a day off or a lengthier vacation (life *will* go on without you), or just putting candles on the table for a special dinner. You know better than anyone else how hard you've worked on your goal. Don't be ashamed to bask in the glow.
- *Dust yourself off when you fall.* Hear me out… you will not always be number one; you will not always get the score or the deal you want. You will fall down every so often, even though you've given it your best. Otherwise, you wouldn't be human. When you do fall, quickly plan your next move, and get on your way. If you lie there and wallow in your failure, you'll only get trampled on more while the game goes on without you. Others will succeed, but you won't. Rely on your own resources and abilities to get the momentum going again. In my training sessions and speeches, I often surprise people with a combat roll – in with my suit on – to dramatically illustrate the point of falling and getting up again. Failure doesn't have to be fatal. Learn to roll with the punches.
- *Identify things that are important to you.* What is important to you

in your life – more free time, being part of a team, having your own home, being in love? Unless you identify what matters to you, how do you expect to become motivated and enthused? You can't. In my life, family, friends and religious faith are the most important things to me. Being successful in my business comes next. Put your own priorities into perspective.
- *Always pay close attention to your basic needs.* Everyone needs love, food, shelter, and friendship. Ensure that your basic needs are met before worrying about ancillary needs.

To use motivation skills effectively, you need to recognize that you can motivate yourself internally as well as externally. Make sure you recognize that:

- *You react differently to the ways that others condition themselves.* You will react differently to your brother than to your sister, and differently to a situation on Monday than you will on Friday. Adapt.
- *You change your behavior over time, not overnight.* The manner in which you behave or react under specific circumstances will change only with time. Adjustment doesn't normally happen instantaneously. Relax.
- *You look for variety in your day and work.* Get out of those ruts that have been eating away at your motivation. There's no time like the present to spice up your repertoire. Create.
- *You want to do worthwhile things.* Worth is the quality within each of us that renders us deserving of respect. Everyone wants to feel worthwhile. Concentrate on the things that are important enough to you to justify an expenditure of time and effort. Select.
- *You want to succeed.* You've got to want success in the first place before you can reach for it. Strive.

As parents generally teach their children, begin at the beginning and take one step at a time. To that I add – keep walking – or you'll never reach your goal.

Successful people succeed because they have the motivation and enthusiasm to forge ahead.

Motivating others

Successful networkers motivate and enthuse not only themselves, but also the people in their networks. It's the ripple effect. If you're motivated and exhibit that you are, your audience, i.e. your network, will get motivated as well. It's a powerful and easy way to lead, and forms the basis of the RIBS "ME" Principle illustrated below.

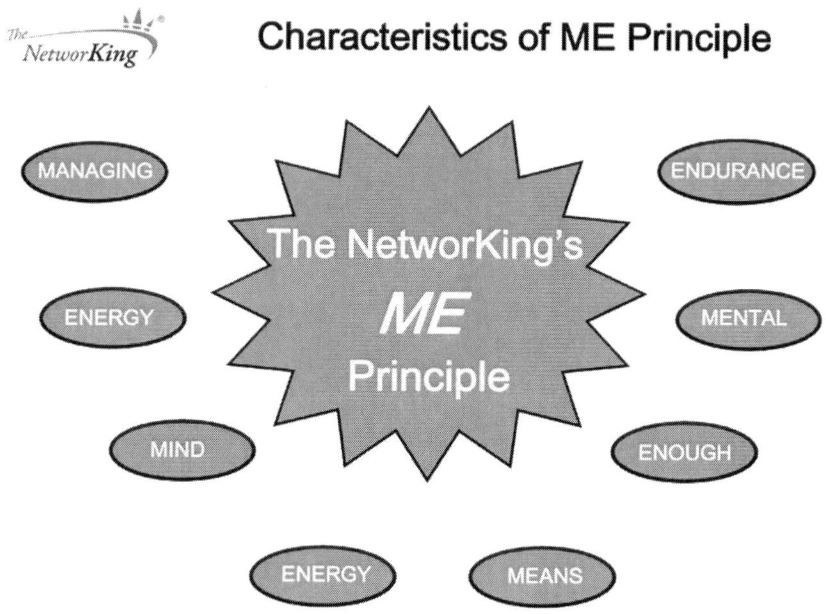

***M**anaging **E**nergy...**M**ind **E**nergy... **M**eans **E**nough **M**ental **E**ndurance*

No excuses, please

There will always be people who complain that they'd be more motivated and enthused if only they could do this or that. Well, the way I look at it, the grass may be greener on the other side of the fence, but thepeople who live there are also paying a much higher water bill.

Everyone has a price to pay. Are you paying too much or too little for your excuses?

Burn, baby burn!

We all have good intentions. In order to capitalize on those good intentions, you need to turn up the heat on your motivation and enthusiasm. Many parents wish that they could do that to theirs teens. Take a good look at yourself for a change, and see where you could stoke your own fire. Full intentions don't get you anywhere unless you light the match on your motivation and enthusiasm.

The intensity of your heat is a measure of how quickly you'll achieve something and *if*, in fact, you'll achieve it at all. You have the ability to unleash a powerful force that will allow you to achieve any goal you set for yourself.

Successful people succeed because they know how to turn up the heat.

Now that you're all fired up, let's take your networking on the road.

"To be successful in your way of networking, it is not enough to have a technique – your personal charm and enthusiasm are the decisive factors.

... In the course of the years, you (Charles) have managed to enthuse masses of people, but some of them will never learn if they don't believe in themselves first."

- Barbara Summa, Madrelingua
The Netherlands

CHAPTER 8:

NETWORKING IN ACTION

"Outings are an untapped reservoir of unlimited resources."

- Charles Ruffolo, The NetworKing

Fishermen go where the fish are. They're prepared with the right information about the lake or stream in which they intend to fish. If they stay home, they catch no fish.

The same thing applies to networking. The fish won't bite unless you go out and cast that line in the proper place.

If this seems calculated, it's because it is. By knowing precisely "who is coming to dinner and where", and then *going* there with a definite plan, you'll be able to hook your network. Whether you want to compare networking to fishing or simply going out on a date, networking outings require preparation in the same way – with conviction, anticipation, energy and enthusiasm.

You've learned how to build your network, communicate to it, expand it, energize it, lead it, and motivate and enthuse it. You're now ready to attempt *networking in action.*

Outings: the core of networking

In my most comprehensive training sessions where I teach individuals or groups of employees how to network, the next to the last session is always an outing. I literally take them out to an event where they can put all they've learned about effective networking into practice while I guide them first-hand. That's why I call these training sessions "HAND Networking Programs". Our last session is a follow-up to that outing to discuss the difficulties and successes they've experienced while networking in action.

- Outings help individuals get more out of networking because:
- Outings are the easiest method of exploring opportunities.
- Outings are the cheapest way of building relationships.
- Outings increase your awareness of movements in the market.
- Outings are filled with an infinite number of business deals and/or social prospects.

Outings can be anywhere where people gather – at the local Chamber of Commerce meetings or luncheons, parties, events or, for that matter, virtually any organization or social function. Because I'm associated with so many different groups, many of which I'm on the board of directors or a particular committee, I'm never at a loss for venues.

It's only logical – you don't meet people and therefore make contacts and therefore network by staying at home. You've simply got to get out there – *somewhere, anywhere* where people gather – Time On Target (T.O.T.), as I learned in the military. In other words, "you 'gotta be there."

Outings are an untapped reservoir of resources that connect you with your intended audience. Truth is, they are the easiest method of exploring opportunities to generate new business, or to connect for success with virtually every need or want that you have. Every outing you attend is filled with literally hundreds, if not thousands, of potential connections.

For business people, outings are the cheapest way to build relationships and, therefore, a client network. They increase awareness of movements in the market, and put people in immediate contact with potential buyers of your products and services. In short, outings are the crux of networking.

Getting there is only half the battle, however. Think about all the various outings that you have been to in the past. Now think about all the opportunities to network that you had at those outings but outright ignored and missed.

Companies send their marketing representatives out to luncheons and dinners hoping that they'll increase business, when typically what happens is that they come back with a full stomach but no new leads. *All* employees, not just sales and marketing personnel, need to learn how to network at outings – and to network in general. They also need to realize that the sales and marketing department is not the entire organization, but the entire organization must be sales and the marketing department.

It's just as important, for example, for secretaries and all support staff to have business cards as it is for the managers and the Chief Executive Officer. In the course of their day, support personnel meet just as many people – perhaps more – than management. Therefore, they are just as capable of networking. You can imagine the positive repercussions for a company when *all* employees network on its behalf.

How to maximize your effectiveness at outings

Once you're at an outing, you need to apply the basic networking principles discussed earlier on in this book. Let's look at how they apply to outings:

The NetworKings 10 Tips for Effective Networking at Outings

1. *Find out where your potential business or personal contacts gather.* That's the first step. Know where your market or target audience assembles, and go there.
2. *Find out as much as you can in advance* about the particular venue and the topic to be addressed so that you have information and knowledge to use and share.
3. *Know who is coming to dinner.* Get a list of attendees through whatever means it takes, e.g. registration, from the host or hostess, on a website, etc., and then study it in advance with your specific goals in mind. Select at least three attendees with whom you intend to link up. Make notes, if preferred, about what you'd like to discuss with each of them.
4. *Be early*. Do you realize what kind of an edge you can have if you arrive early to an event? First of all, it gives you an opportunity to pick up the registration list, if you don't already have one, in order to plan your networking. Secondly, it gives you the opportunity to select your seat, if they haven't already been assigned (in which case you could try to get it changed) so that you CHOOSE by whom you will sit. Remember, your time is limited. Determine whom you need to sit next to and take the initiative to make sure it happens. If you are not yet acquainted with the particular person(s), ask the organizer or host(ess) of the event to point that person out to you as he or she arrives (therein lies another reason to be early), introduce yourself as soon as you can and lead your selected audience to his or her seat. (This is all part of leading your network.) If the event involves a lunch or dinner, guide the person to his or her seat after the opening reception. In the meantime, network! You don't need to wait until the event actually gets off the ground to begin networking. On the contrary, networking begins outside the front door, so go early and get a head start. You'll need the extra time. By arriving early, you can also get a good parking place and

help to set up. While we're on the subject of seats, let me point out that you should never sit with your back to the crowd. By arranging to sit with maximum face-to-face exposure, you'll be able to see who's talking to whom and scope out your target audience. Targets are generally moving targets, so you've got to keep on your toes. Sit where you can see who's coming and going. After all, you need to be prepared to run out of the room if that elusive person you wanted to meet decides to leave early.

5. *There are no strangers, only friends you have not met.* As I've said previously, your best friend or partner was once a stranger. For more reticent people, connecting with strangers can be daunting. If you expect to network your way to success, however, you've got to lift the veil. By far the best thing I ever did was to have the nerve to introduce myself, years ago, to that beauty in the boutique who is now my wife Herma. Open your own life up to the opportunities afforded by connecting with strangers. You'll be amazed where it will lead.
6. *For results, sit by a stranger.* This follows in line with number four above and deserves more emphasis. What do most people do when they attend an outing of some sort? You've got it! They sit by a friend or colleague. What good does that do besides afford you an opportunity to chat with your buddy? Not much, but it sure impedes networking, which should be the primary reason you came. Tell your friends that you'll see them after the event for a coffee or a drink, that you have "work" to do at this event – "net-work". If you haven't carefully selected your target audience to sit next to, choose a stranger – any stranger – and find the link between the two of you. Trust me, there is one. Whatever you do, don't wallow in a comfort zone.
7. *Use the five-minute rule.* For the most effective, high-powered networking at events, allow an average of five minutes per interaction. That way you can scour the room for as many available links as possible. Let's be realistic here, however. If you've just linked up with the one person who you think can potentially change your life, the priorities change. But if you're looking to get the maximum out of networking, expand your business and/or promote yourself, the five-minute rule should apply. With your list in hand, simply excuse yourself from the ongoing conversation by pointing out that you

have several people you must connect with before the event is over, then circulate.

8. *Apply effective listening.* As I've said before, it's often easier to talk about yourself than to listen – truly listen – to others. What you miss when you tune out may be the very thing you need to hear. Practice effective listening. Stay in the present; don't be eyeing your next contact or thinking about your next sentence. You'll lose out, guaranteed. As Albert Einstein once said, "If A is a success in life, then A equals X plus Y plus Z. Work is X, Y is play, and Z is keeping your mouth shut."

The illustration below presents the power of listening as it relates to overall communications. Notice that after two days, you only retain 25% of what you have heard.

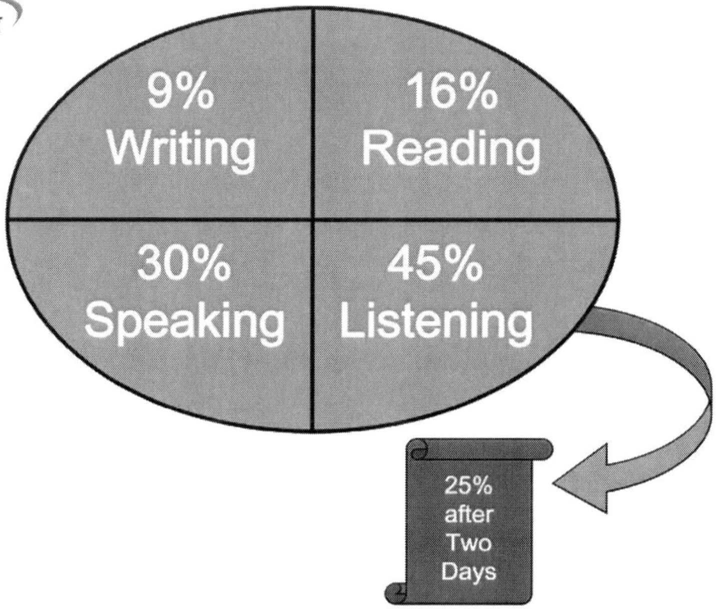

9. *Be enthusiastic.* Let's face it, no one likes a sourpussed drone. Exhibit some life in your demeanor; smile, extend your hand in an enthusiastic manner and come across as someone who enjoys life, even if it happens to be hard to pull it off that day. If you radiate pleasantness and enthusiasm, you'll radiate success. Just don't overdo it, however, or your enthusiasm may backfire. Walk the fine line, but lean toward the positive.
10. *Thank the master of ceremonies, speaker and/or host(ess) – as well as the service personnel.* There isn't a person on earth that doesn't like to be thanked. It's a simple gesture that only takes 15 seconds more of your time. Before you walk out that door, thank the appropriate person(s) for his or her contribution to the event. Not only will you be doing a good deed, but also you'll be continuing to network right up to the end, and often with the most important person there. End on a high note. And don't be duped into thinking that that waiter or waitress serving your table isn't important. He or she may go on to be the hospitality manager one day – and this has actually happened in my experience, and I currently deal with that person on a regular basis at the hotel where I hold some of my training seminars. Besides, *everyone* deserves recognition and appreciation. Dole it out generously.

Make outings work for you

Outings are the heart of networking. Plan for them on a regular basis. They are the culmination of all your preparation, and the catalyst that will get your network up and running.

As an aside here, please don't ever use the excuse that you are too busy to network. If you're busy, you *are* networking. You've just got to do it consciously. Make conscious networking a priority in your life. Networking eventually becomes an unconscious routine that feels like it doesn't take up any more of your time at all. And in fact, it doesn't.

Your next mission

Congratulations! You now know how to network. Almost. You haven't gone full circle until you also give back.

And if you think that you can just skip the next chapter on giving back, think again. You may as well burn this book and forget everything that you've learned if you think that giving back is not a necessary part of networking. Giving back is that critical to networking success.

So then, on to the next chapter.

"He (Ruffolo) will push you to actively do business rather than wait politely for it to fall into your lap... his eye-popping lack of inhibition is one of his most valuable assets... Totally unhandicapped by any form of shyness himself, he vaporizes any reticence within a 500-meter radius."

- Cathy Scott, as quoted from her article in the June/July issue of Expats Magazine, published by Aromedia Print, Amsterdam

CHAPTER 9:

GIVING TO YOUR NETWORK

"The cardinal rule of networking is giving back. Without it, there is no relationship and therefore no network."

- Charles Ruffolo, The NetworKing and Founder, Giving Back Foundation

Have you ever read the novel *Pay it Forward* by Catherine Ryan Hyde (2000), or seen the movie of the same name based on the book? If so, you'll know the power that giving can have, of paying someone back – or forward, as the case may be.

Essentially, what goes around comes around. Give and you shall receive. Do unto others… No matter how you slice it, giving back is powerful—and a proven mechanism for overall success.

The power of giving to your network is enormous. Giving back is absolutely essential to networking. In fact, I believe it's so essential that in 1999 I founded a charitable organization, or *Stichting* as they call it here in The Netherlands: the Giving Back Foundation, started with the help and encouragement of John Padget and Buford Alexander, who gave Giving Back its name. Both of them have become not only strong business associates, but close friends and supporters of the Foundation.

With that in mind, let's take a look at how *giving back* to your own network can make such a difference.

The seesaw effect

Everyone's been on a seesaw – that ingeniously simple playground device that goes up and down as the weight of two people shifts. Picture networking in the same way. What flows up flows down; what goes out comes back; what is given is gained. Reciprocity is key.

But hang on to your hats! As with a seesaw, you can't pump your network too fast or you'll bump the other person off. Networking has to have a gentle rhythm of give and receive. If you fly off the handle and *take* too much, your "playmate" will jump off the seesaw and disappear. A network can NEVER be one-sided, i.e. only for your benefit, or it just won't work. After all, no one likes a leech. You cannot just call on your network when you need it.

If you never remember anything else about networking, remember this: networking will *not* work unless you give back. If you only focus on getting, your resources will eventually dry up in reaction to your self-focused motives.

Aren't we only giving to get?

If you are only giving to get, wake up and smell the bitter coffee. Number one, it's fair to say that it's unethical. Number two, your network will die a slow death. Number three, you won't benefit from the inward satisfaction that giving provides.

Take it from me, there's no better way to glow from the inside out than to help others. The feeling is incomparable. In fact, it's a real high – and long lasting.

The reality is this: if you don't provide an equal balance to your networking, the incoming connections and resources will eventually trickle down to a slow leak. No one wants to deal with a person who only takes and doesn't give back. You will eventually become very unpopular, untrustworthy and avoided. The real tango doesn't start until you offer your hand in kind.

In other words, *a relationship is not a relationship until you give in return.* This concept is so vital to me that my Giving Back Foundation, a charitable organization that I founded in 1999 whereby volunteers provide career-mentoring programs for minority students residing in The Netherlands (see Appendix), has adopted a special handshake, illustrated on the front cover, that implies that while you have been given a hand to reach your goals, the finger points back to you because the onus is on *you* to succeed. Both persons' index fingers point at the other, directing the focus, as it were, on the recipient, as opposed to one's self. The volunteer work that we do via this foundation has given me more in terms of feeling good about my life than any amount of dollars or euros could ever give.

Since her foundation in 1999, The Giving Back Foundation continues to grow immensely, you can read all about in The Afterword.

The following by-words of my Giving Back Foundation are applicable to people in all walks of life, not only to our participating students:

- *Hope* (Faith and courage hope to reach goals)
- *Responsibility* (Owning up to your actions)
- *Respect* (Realizing that it's earned, not given)

- *Enthusiasm (*Enjoying the things you do in life)
- *Generosity* (Learning to give back)

By employing these values and "giving back" on a regular basis, you'll be amazed at the results. In fact, the *less* you expect in return, the *more* you will actually receive. It happens all the time. If you get in the habit of doing *for* others, the equation will always balance out. The seesaw will always come back down. You can count on it.

I contend that we all need a purpose in life, a way of helping others, no matter how big or small. Whatever your interest or passion or business, you should be able to find some way to give back. To me, it's worth every minute of time spent.

I know from experience, however, that you must give without an agenda for results. That's the difference. Besides, if you get in the habit of giving of yourself, good things in life will automatically flow back to you. Of that there is no doubt.

How networks grow from giving back

From early on in my childhood, I saw that many people from all walks of life were volunteering in our local community and business world in order to "do good" for others and to get to know each other, thereby increasing their network. Whether it was in church, at school or for the local scouting organization, volunteers were providing help for free.

As an Alter Boy at my parish church, for example, I gave back and participated in a church network. I saw my father volunteering on the sports field as the local football coach. Everyone in turn knew who I was – especially when the home team was winning – and a basic network was formed.

At school, volunteering was very evident. Moms and dads gave of their time to help out in numerous ways with bake sales, fieldtrips and fundraisers. A network was formed.

My father also served as president of the local chapter of the Fraternal Order of the Eagles (F.O.E.) where he volunteered his time and got his brothers and friends to participate and give back to the community. A network was formed.

Numerous family members served on local club committees or boards, volunteering their services in such organizations as the Veterans of Foreign Wars (V.F.W.), and the Knights of Columbus. Vast networks were formed.

In the military, I learned teamwork and camaraderie. Believe me, there's no better example of the repercussions of not supporting each other than what could happen behind a battle line. It's the same on the street and in your network as it is in the trenches. Take care of the people in your network, and they'll take care of you.

In the business world, volunteering or giving back is visible in the various Chambers of Commerce, numerous service organizations, trade associations and other civic and charitable groups. More often than not, these organizations are the central point of the business community where innumerable contacts can be made just by becoming involved. Joining and volunteering in such organizations gives you a voice in your community, enables you to give back, and provides an endless stream of contacts and resources. As a member, you will be added to the directory, a network in itself. But more importantly, it's what you *do* as a member that provides the vital link to a particular network. Divvy up some of your valuable time to volunteer in some capacity, and you'll ultimately see both civic *and* networking results.

Joining local clubs, for example, multiplies your chances to effectively network in your community by providing you with the structure and opportunity to volunteer. Being part of a professional organization will help you show your leadership skills and to focus and assist with the important issues facing you both. It's your willingness to serve and eventually chair or be a member of a committee, however, that gives you the networking visibility and edge that you need to energize those networks.

Committee work provides a vital link to other members and resources. A great place to sit is on an organization's membership committee where you get a chance to interact with incoming and current members in a direct way. What better position than to network with those with like interests and unlimited networks of their own? In the same breath, your willingness to give back enables you to help your community and your business world to grow and prosper.

If you don't see any function or committee to which you would naturally be suited, create one. Be proactive and establish an outlet for your particular expertise. And, yes, you do have some kind of expertise. Everyone has a gilded vein running through his or her body. Where is yours?

There's nothing wrong with carefully selecting the organizations and clubs that will give you the most return on your networking investment. You'll still be helping your community in some way, shape or form. Those in a similar line of business or focus of interest will be obvious choices for you. Likewise, select those to which you have more to offer, depending on your skills and talents. Then give back – or shall we say forward – and you'll discover how the boomerang will come back every time.

The more you give, the more you'll receive. It happens by osmosis.

Bartering your services

This may seem like a strange place to include the concept of bartering – of exchanging services instead of cash – but I feel that it belongs here because it's a perfect way to give back without incurring financial debt on either side of the equation. I barter all the time. In fact, I probably accomplish more things by bartering my time and services than any other way.

Many people are initially turned off by the concept of bartering, but if it's worked for centuries, it can, and does, still work today. Just consider how easy it might be for you to say to someone, "Look, I can't pay you for your service, but I can do something for you in return." That's bartering.

Keep the valuable concept of bartering in your back pocket as a way of not only receiving what you want or need, but as a way of giving back your time, your attention, your services and your expertise.

Plug in your assets

Your network – our world and society, no less – needs your philanthropic efforts. Figure out what you can do for someone else before you figure out what they can do for you. In fact, the more you concentrate on the former, the more the latter will just fall into your lap.

Be confident about what you have to offer. Know your assets, and network those assets to your network. Everyone has something to give. If you truly don't know what that might be in your case, a quick way to find out is to ask your friends, family or colleagues for their opinion. They'll quickly tell you what your strengths (and perhaps your weaknesses!) are. Sometimes we can't see those strengths ourselves. Use their objective mirror.

Once you figure out what that strength is for you, give back to your community in the most appropriate way you can. The experience of helping someone else achieve what they want or need in life is highly gratifying.

As Winston Churchill so aptly said, "You make a living by what you get; you make a life by what you give."

Networking will flow naturally from all your humanitarian efforts. It's a given.

"Giving Back has become very important for me. Not only was I immediately enthusiastic about the idea, it turns out that the whole Giving Back team is something special .... Ruf is the reason for that.

Ruf is the most enthusiastic person promoting Giving Back... I mean, have you ever seen someone doing push-ups on a stage just to get sponsorship money?

I believe that Giving Back is still going strong because of this crazy, special man. He just loves people in a very authentic and sincere way.

Ruf IS Giving Back!"

-Gladys Frijmersum, Director, Imola Executive Search,
Giving Back Mentor and Volunteer, The Netherlands

In his own words...

A tribute from Michael Bell,
Michael Bell ExecSelect, The Netherlands

Amsterdam, 22 September 2003

I guess I've known Ruf about 12 or 13 years. My earliest recollections of him stem from the time I was still a director with the FedEx Corporation here in Europe. As such, I was very active within the American business community and Ruf was in the process of retiring from the U.S. Army after 20 years of service. He used to come up to Amsterdam or The Hague and participate in many of the events organized by the American Chamber of Commerce (AmCham) – part of his reintegration process. One thing about Ruf, the network skill he now demonstrates so ably was honed in the Army.

In particular, I remember Ruf from one of the early AmCham Annual Golf Tournaments. He was obviously impressed and let it be known. As time went by and he finally did retire from the military, he steadily became a regular fixture of all our business activities. As one of the longest-serving members of the Amsterdam American Business Club, when I was asked to establish a board of directors and become it's first official president, it was only natural to think of including a guy like Ruf. The rest is history.

But that's not my finest reminiscence; no, that's from another time. In 1997 my father passed away after a long battle with cancer. I went back to the United States for the funeral held at Arlington National Cemetery. My dad had served almost 30 years in the U.S. Marine Corps and was given a very impressive send-off. It made a big impression on me and while I had grown up in a Marine Corps family, my dad was a quiet type who seldom talked about his military experiences.

When my mother starting cleaning up the house, she came across his service medals, which had been carefully stored away but were all still in their individual boxes. She duly sent them off to me with a note that she didn't know the proper order they were supposed to be in, but perhaps I could inquire at one of the U.S. military installations here in Europe.

The first person I turned to for help was Ruf. Of course he offered to assist, and was only too happy to take a plastic bag full of medals off my hands, saying he would see what he could do. Several weeks later I got a call letting me know that I could pick the medals up at the U.S. Army Base at Schinnen down in Limburg. I did find it strange when Ruf asked if I was aware of what my dad had for medals – I said I really wasn't too sure. When I got down to Schinnen I was met by one of Ruf's many friends (Angelo Borelli) and, to my absolute amazement, was handed a beautifully mounted and framed set of medals. I hadn't asked for or expected something like this, but it was such a kind gesture and so professionally done that my first reaction was to ask how much it would cost. You can imagine the lump in my throat and tear in my eye when I was told it was an honor to have the privilege to mount the medals free for a serviceman thus decorated.

This is just one of the many things that Ruf has 'been there for' that I could relate, and it will stick with me and my family for generations to come.

I would just like to close by saying to Ruf on behalf of my dad, "Semper Fi " – and thanks.

Michal Bell
Michael Bell ExecSelect
The Netherlands

CHAPTER 10:

PROFESSIONALIZING YOUR NETWORK WITH THE NETWORKING, RIBS NETWORK AND THE NETWORK CLUB

"In one evening, my Network Club events bring hundreds of people in touch with literally thousands of valuable connections."

- Charles Ruffolo, The NetworKing

Who would have ever guessed that a small-town, ruffian from Pittsburgh, Pennsylvania would be earning a good living as a self-proclaimed Professional Networker based in the Netherlands?

Today, I have not one but three organizations devoted to networking and giving back: RIBS (Ruffolo International Business Services) Network, begun in 1995, which facilitates connections among business people and through which I give speeches and conduct custom-tailored network training sessions; The Networking B.V., started in 2008, a professional networking organization, bringing businesses closer together and helping nurture profitable and meaningful business relationships;

The Network Club, started in 1999, which currently has over 3,000 members, providing valuable contacts, networking venues and news; The NetworKing Academy, started in 2010, where in a 3-month program participants learn to develop their personal networking skills to become a professional networker; and my non-profit charity, the Giving Back Foundation, whereby mentors help minority high-school students in the Netherlands by exploring career options with them.

In 2000, I held my first Network Club event in Amsterdam with 110 people in attendance. Today those events, which take place eight times a year throughout the Netherlands, attract three times that amount and help people to expand and *professionalize* their own network. Plans to expand with franchises to the rest of Europe and the United States are already being formulated.

My secret?

My prescription for success

As a Professional Networker, I have the oldest profession in the world. I know you're thinking that there's an older one, but let me clear up that misunderstanding right away.

Before any sparks ever flew in that other profession, the original partners had to connect by means of a network, but unlike the chicken and the egg dilemma, we know for a fact that the network had to come first. Everything else followed – including bonding and giving. So you see, my profession *is* the oldest.

In all seriousness, though, I'd have to say that motivation and enthusiasm (ME) are at the heart of my success. I eat, sleep and breathe networking, and anyone who knows me will tell you that it's an understatement to say that I'm motivated and enthused. I've turned networking into a science and a business. Everything I do is based on networking. I earn money by doing what I love to do. I have no products on a shelf, only people in my network, and I make a living by connecting people who have things in common and energizing my network to give back.

I'm also direct. People think, for example, that if they just get up in front of the person making a decision on something they they'll make a sale. I tell them flat out that they could have the best product, the best price, the most reliable service, and the most intervened system, but if the chemistry is not right between the two of them, they are *not* going to do business together. As you are now aware, you must first build a rapport and a relationship based on trust, respect, faith and honesty – bonding with your network.

I too had the wrong perspective early on, despite all the determination in the world, about becoming a success. While I was doing my jumping jacks in the military at "O-Dark thirty" in the morning and getting my Master's degree in the evening and on the weekends, I thought all it took was to be both book smart and street smart to make my way in the business world. I had never sold anything or marketed a new product, and never motivated anyone, up to that point, to reach his or her goal, other than my fellow soldiers to get home alive.

The difference was, I was goal oriented, task driven, motivated and "stress managed", as I call it, regardless of the mission. Also, I was always on time, and was accustomed to working as a team player as a soldier and officer. I thought I'd "have it made in the shade" in terms of entering the business world. What I didn't realize is that I was missing the most vital key of all: a *network*. I thought I'd get a job in the business world without any trouble – heck, I had all the credentials on paper – but I did *not* have the proper network.

Once I realized that necessity, I was on my way to success. Not only that, I turned my realization into my life's work. I created my own networking profession out of an ideal that I believed in very deeply. In fact, I've gone so far with this concept that today my designation as "The Networ-King" is even trademarked, and I've now published this book on my own "product" of networking.

Another reason that I'm successful, I believe, is that people know that I mean what I say and that I can be relied upon to come through on my commitments. I mince no words, but I always speak with enthusiasm, sincerity and respect.

Also, I'm successful because my extended network excludes no one… and I mean no one. That's the crucial difference, perhaps, between me and other networkers. I'm fortunate enough to have a sufficient ream of family and close friends, but those close to me know that it took time to build that rapport. Good relationships, like good networks, don't just happen overnight; they must be nurtured. Before I invite someone over for a BBQ or become a good friend, our relationship has to grow and develop. But as far as my extended network goes, I can *never* have enough people there. It's obvious to those around me that the circumference of that circle is boundless.

Above all, networking is a way of life for me. Before I lift my head rises off the pillow every morning, I'm already networking in my mind. My data file extends from one corner of the earth to the other and, as my family and relations know, networking is my lifeblood. It motivates and enthuses me to succeed, and to spread my success among others.

Some people say that being American has a lot to do with my style and success. Well, to that I reply that my father came from Italy, and I've lived in the Netherlands since 1976, so that shoots a few holes in that theory. On the contrary, I'm an expatriate who has absorbed the Dutch culture and language (although many would disagree with that, knowing how I speak Dutch and English together), and I despise stereotypes. Believe me, there's nobody more "red, white and blue" than I am, but I simply deny the claim that being an outgoing American makes me a better networker. As I've emphasized early on in this book, *anyone* can network… the same as I do.

No, I am who I am. I'm here to do business, and I like to give back. My actions speak louder than my words. If you need help, ask me to help, and I will. Invite me where you need me and I'll be there. I'll teach anyone and everyone how to network for success – not because I'm American, but because it's a way of life for me and I'm passionate about it. And if you apply what you've learned in the previous chapters, you'll no doubt have the same reaction and results as I do.

Think about the myriad networks that you automatically possess just by virtue of getting up in the morning: your immediate family and your extended family, your neighbors, your friends, your community and your colleagues. Now think about the exponential value to you, as we've discussed, of all *their* networks.

By virtue of this book, you now know how to look beyond that box with the silver spoon in it. You know how to build, communicate to, expand, energize, lead, motivate and enthuse, network in action and give back to your network. If you practice these methods religiously, they'll become routine to you, and you'll be networking for life, as automatically and unconsciously as you probably pedal a bike. There shouldn't be any facet of your life that isn't affected in a positive way by networking. Once you energize your network, there's no turning back. You won't be able to turn off the tap; and the benefits to you and others to whom you give back will pour forth.

This book serves as a launching pad for you. I'd also like to provide you with access to my on-line Network Club, as well as my regular networking events and training sessions. Such events, which take place on a regular basis in The Netherlands where I reside, can be arranged virtually anywhere in the world with sufficient advance notice.

All of these activities are detailed at length on my websites at www.TheNetworkClub.com, www.TheNetworKing.com and www.ribs.nl. In the meantime, here are some specifics.

The Network Club

My on-line Network Club, which now receives more than several million hits per year, grew out of necessity. People were calling me constantly for someone's telephone number. They called me looking for connections for jobs. They called me because they have a job and they need to find an employee. They called me because they have something to sell. They called me because they were trying to do business in the Netherlands, or the States, or wherever, and they need to know whom to contact and where to start.

The Network Club is the device I came up with to address all those needs... and more. It was generated from a conversation I had with my best friend, Martijn de Looze, while sitting at his home brainstorming about how to use my network to earn money. That day, we mapped out the concept and outlined my ideas for using the Internet and events to energize my network and that of others. We still talk about our foresight.

Today, The Network Club is a fast growing club dedicated to facilitating business by providing a platform for members to establish, strengthen and utilize personal relationships for mutual success. More and more, companies are realizing the importance of the human dimension to doing business. Indeed, tapping into new markets, opportunities or knowledge depends largely on relationships with external parties.

The Network Club membership, which is based on information sharing, represents a diverse group of people from all vertical markets and, at this writing, includes over 3,000 members worldwide who have one aim in mind: networking. In addition to many other benefits, the site provides members with direct access to a niche market of North American and European business people who rely on up-to-date information and contacts. It gives participating companies and individuals the opportunity to acquire new clients, strengthen existing customer relationships, and motivate employees to do more business.

By clicking on my site, you too can have access to all other Network Club members' information. Twenty-four hours a day, you can stay abreast of what's going on in a highly diverse network. As a platform for members and sponsors on which to market, advertise and promote their services and products to a wide and varied audience, its effectiveness is clear.

When you visit my site, you'll see how easy it is to search for other members that you may want to contact and be privy to their relevant information provided with that aim in mind. You can also view member discounts, job postings, classified ads, mini-websites, members' events, special member features *and*, if you become a member, post your own resume/CV, job offerings, classifieds, discounts, Websites, features and services or products.

Major Sponsors from all walks of business and private sectors invest their time and money in my site and my events. Why? Because it works. I provide the platform, and get a powerful resource.

If members do business as a result, great. If they earn money from it, even better. And if they, in turn give back ... well, I couldn't ask for more

Needless to say, The Network Club represents a goldmine of opportunities for networking. On average, 225 business-minded people currently attend my networking events, from such organizations as Canon, ACN, Sprint, Citibank, Microsoft, US Airways, NFL Europe, ZaZare Diamonds, Marriott Hotel, Delta Air Lines, MCI, Ernst & Julio Gallo Winery, and ABN-AMRO Bank. So can you.

Announcements of upcoming Network Club venues, which currently take place eight times a year throughout The Netherlands – *plus* family days and other social events – are always posted on the site, with several months advance notice and on-line registration. Everything you need to know to plan your specific networking at these events is right there in front of you, including a roster of who will be attending each event, with short biographies available on those members attending – a perfect way to determine your target audience for the outing. For virtually all events, there's even a carpool service provided by the attending members themselves and, in many instances, by me personally.

In short, everything you need to energize your network through The Network Club is provided. How much easier can it be? By simply clicking on a particular member profile, you can send an e-mail or access phone number. You'll also have valuable information at hand to use when you do meet members face-to-face at one of my Network Club events – their attendance at which, I might add, you can also ascertain through the registration list that I post for each event. The platform is there; all you need to do is become a member, show up at the events with your business card and conviction, your partners and guests, and use the compete range of resources.

- Membership is offered in three levels, with different rates (check the site for current rates) as follows:
- Enterprise Member – membership with the most benefits
- Business Member- membership with moderate benefits
- Entrepreneur – membership with fewer benefits

Companies or individuals who want to get the most mileage out of their membership can be a sponsor, giving them the added benefit of posting their own ads on The Network Club website, as well as maximum exposure at all Network Club events.

The big events!

Word has it that I'm not known for being reserved, and my Network Club events reflect my unbridled enthusiasm and energy. When I'm in action, I'm hitting on every cylinder. Only by being there can one comprehend how I link the 200-300 people typically at these events. With my high-speed, Rolodex mind, I connect people I know with those I discover *in situ*, linking them through that proven networking force of common bonds. The action on the floor is feverish but the precision – military.

Bonds are forged, friendships made, and business deals initiated. I lay the platform, remove the obstacles, make it fun, encourage the links, and the rest is up to those who attend. If the evening is not fruitful, those attending have only themselves to blame because the connections are there. The Network Club events are truly an unparalleled opportunity for members and their invited guests to expand their markets and network for success.

As participants arrive, they are given a list of attendees. For those networkers who haven't already sited that out on my website beforehand, this vital tool is conveniently provided.

The program for each event is essentially the same – we start at 6 PM and end at 10 PM. Everything in between is arranged by me in advance for our members and invited guests, and everything is free: location, catering, entertainment, name tags, attendees list, prizes, gifts, parking… you name it. Why? Because I want members to come to my Network Club events with one thing in mind and one thing only – doing business, i.e. networking. There's no entry fee, no hidden cost, no gimmick, only networking and giving back to each other. In the four hours of these events, there are literally thousands of networking opportunities to tap into. That's a lot of resources – and potential networks – in one room. As you can see, it all adds up to a networking opportunity and very enjoyable social event … and all you have to do is sign up and get yourself there.

Here's how the evening takes shape. First, I welcome everyone at the door and shake his of her hand, honouring them as my guests. Then we enjoy a lavish buffet of food and complimentary drinks – based on a lesson I learned from my military days about the importance of a hot meal after a day's battle. Many people drive a very long distance to attend my events – with some even coming from other countries – and I want to be sure that their stomachs are full before we get down to business.

Throughout this time, my wife Herma sings (and yes, she really *can* sing… singing is only one of the careers that she has, the other one being a Justice of the Peace who joins people in marriage). After that I give a solid but, at the same time entertaining presentation on networking fundamentals, thereby setting the stage for networking in action. The action really begins as I "work the floor" and feverishly match individuals in the audience who I know have a connection of which they themselves are probably not aware. One thing leads to another, and many rapid-fire bonds are forged.

As the action heats up and attendees get the idea, I present to them a Networking in Action Challenge whereby each person has 90 minutes to network with three people in the room, based on the attendees list that the he or she received upon arrival. The goal, of course, is to network, proven by getting those three people to sign a card that I provide. This Networking in Action "toolcard" is then used in a drawing for several major prizes generously donated by my sponsors. Ultimately, everyone is a winner because, in addition to great prizes (just ask The Network Club regulars), no one goes home without valuable connections.

By the same token, money is raised at every event for the Giving Back Foundation, and a further 10% of what I earn on The Network Club memberships is donated to either the Nationaal Fonds Kinderhulp organization, the Glen Mills School, or the Giving Back Foundation, according to each member's choice – a way of giving back in return.

Never been? Skeptical? I challenge you to come to one of my events and not enjoy yourself, or to go away without several important new networks. It won't happen. I'm that confident about the power of these events.

HAND Networking training program

As a Professional Networker, I wanted to add further credibility to my profession, so, in addition to my Network Club website and events, I created a training program on networking and brought that into the market for organizations, companies, universities, schools, and institutions. I call it my "HAND Networking Program" because in business a handshake implies a deal; you meet new people with a handshake; you give someone a hand when they reach their goals; and you salute in the military with a hand salute stating that you bear no arms. Handshakes are an important symbol to me of bonding, so much so that the cover of my book reflects its relevance and significance. (And yes that's Herma, my wife, shaking hands with me.)

My training program was designed to increase self-confidence and empower people to network by focusing on how to tap into and energize different networks, with the primary aim of gaining a larger segment of the market.

These are the objectives of my HAND Networking Program:

1. To give participants a HAND to help them reach their goals and objectives.
2. To ensure that the participants clearly understand that reaching their goals and objectives is in their HANDS only.
3. To help participants maintain a good working relationship with existing customers.
4. To help participants increase services and selling products to these existing customers.
5. To help participants increase sales by penetrating and tapping into new markets.
6. To help participants increase in-house knowledge exchange in order to leverage this knowledge to the company's advantage.
7. To teach participants how to apply the HAND skills learned in order to energize their networks.
8. To guide participants in exploring different networks.
9. To assist participants in profiting from effective networking.
10. To encourage participants to have fun in what they do, and to give back to their networks.

Networking is obviously the main focus of my Hand Networking Program. The objective is to "to help, or benefit from contacts with individuals with whom participants have a direct or indirect relationship, in a positive process of mutual support" – the very essence of my networking creed.

Because an essential characteristic of a leading company or organization is, among others, that its employees and representatives be well trained and well disciplined, training is vital. Discipline derives and flows from training and serves to emphasize the fact that training is all encompassing, permeating everything a company does.

My HAND Networking Program provides individuals with a powerful networking foundation upon which they can build and increase their ability to effectively profit from networking. By preparing themselves to learn more about current customers and potential business relations, as well as previously untapped knowledge within the company, participants forge an entirely new direction that enables them to network their way to success.

The HAND Networking Program is based on the mission, goal and ambitions of a particular organization or group. It involves time, people, equipment, facilities, money and the wisdom to determine precisely what training needs to be done. Since most of these factors are in a constant state of flux, training must be carefully planned and managed.

To further ensure an effective training program, my fundamental The NetworKing's 8 P Principle, addressed in Chapter 2, is set forth:

P*roper* - **P***rior* - **P***LANNING* - **P***revents* - **P***iss* - **P***oor* - **P***ROFIT* - **P***erformance*

This principle is applied toward improving performance at the various levels of an organization, specifically as we discuss Individual Skills, the Collective Effort, and the Company, and how combining these elements will help them reach their collective goals and ambitions.

Specific elements of the HAND Networking Program are:

* The **"Art of Networking"**, a session that focuses on establishing, recognizing, energizing and managing your network. Individuals learn to link basic management principles of directing, organizing, controlling, communicating and planning to energize their network.
* The **"Art of Motivation & Enthusiasm"** (ME), a session that focuses on identifying and recognizing the elements necessary to motivate one's self and other networks. Individuals learn how to approach a situation in an enthusiastic manner, and why enthusiasm is a powerful factor in daily life and in doing business.
* The ***''Art of Communicating to Your Network"***, a session that focuses on getting the message across very clearly and effectively to your network. Communicating accurately, specifically, and stating the goals as simply as possible, by using the right language without hidden meanings.
* The ***''Art of Leading Your Network"***, a session that focuses on leadership as the ability to inspire someone to succeed within your network, involving an understanding of the human dimension, i.e. the ability to apply personal attributes (values, norms, moral character, beliefs, morals, ethical standards, etc.).
* ***"Networking In Action"***, a session that focuses on taking individuals directly into an actual business outing and showing first hand how to apply the skills of networking to a practical setting. The

business outings selected provide a wider view of the market and allow individuals to put their networking skills into action.

* ***"Bridging the Gap"***, an evaluation and feedback portion of the program, with overall goal of improving performance at each level within the organization. Individuals are the key element in the Program.

Individual training is the foundation upon which a company's effectiveness is built. It is the source of individual confidence and trust in an organization. Individual training provides continuity and contributes to sustaining individuals and company effectiveness, as well as to reinforcing an individual's confidence in his or her overall ability to succeed.

If you're interested in either participating or organizing one of these training sessions, you may want to check some of the references that are featured on my dedicated Website at www.TheNetworKing.com

Results achieved from HAND Networking Program

There are several advantages to this training program as designed. The sense of reinforcement and sustainment of individual and collective training throughout the year is apparent. While progression from session to session is recommended, not required, it is clear that the synergism of the full program is immeasurable.

Participants in the HAND Networking Program must learn early on not to think of training as the insatiable enemy that endlessly consumes his/her time, but as that of a tool used to hone and polish their skills and knowledge. It should, however, be regarded as an effective way to align employee expectations with company priorities.

Individuals participating in the HAND Networking Program can expect to achieve these results:

1. Experience first hand that networking is a skill that works – that it's also easy, fun, and free, and that everyone can do it effectively with the proper training.

2. To stay ahead of the market curve, take control of situations, spot opportunities early on, focus on the customer and reach business targets by effectively networking.

3. Gain expertise by focusing more on:
   Knowing your network
   Targeting your network
   Selling to your network
   Maximizing internal knowledge transfer/sharing

4. Experience first hand at business outings that networking is a way of life, and that everyone does it without even thinking about its power.

5. Learn to effectively energize their networks by finding common ground and giving back to their networks.

6. Acquire a powerful networking foundation that they can build upon and thereby increase their ability to effectively profit from networking.

Individual confidence, empowerment and competency develop throughout the HAND Networking Program. Levels increase over time by actively participating in a carefully-designed progression of networking sessions, experience exchanges and individually initiated activities.

Individual development unfolds in each of the networking sessions by providing a continuing cycle of education, training, experience, assessment, feedback and reinforcement that guarantees a level of appreciation for the power of networking.

WRAPPING IT UP

In 10 chapters, you've learned all the basics of networking: how to build, communicate to, expand, energize, lead, motivate, enthuse, network in action, and give back to and professionalize your network You should now be convinced, as I am, of it's power. Combined with The NetworKing, my HAND Networking Program, The Network Club and Giving Back Foundation forums, you have every networking tool you could ever need.

So what are you waiting for? Get out there and energize your network.

As you put down this book and make your way for the door, however, remember two things if nothing else: Who you know is not as important as who knows *you*; and the cardinal rule of networking is giving back.

Peek out your window, then. There's a stranger out there with a connection that could change your life. Get that silver spoon out of the drawer and feed your network.

You've got the power. Now *Network Your Way to Success*.

"Too often I have been to a meeting of another network organization and people exchange business cards and the speaker will encourage networking, however when it comes down to it, nothing really happens. People have lunch, say a few polite words to each other and then leave again.

Ruf's events are completely different. During his events, he almost forces people to network by 'Ruf working the floor', and by calling people up to the stage to give them a chance to highlight their assets or their product, service or company. After that, he links these people if he feels that a potential business relationship can be built.

Watching Ruf work the floor is incredible. That guy doesn't stand still. He'll talk to your for about 20 seconds and then move on to the next person or introduce you to someone else – all in a very pleasant way.

Furthermore, his follow-up is remarkable. Sometimes he even calls me to say, 'Hey, Rob, did you ever call that person I told you about last time? You guys should do business together!'

Ruf truly lives and breathes what he preaches which, in my experience, is very unique. I have never met anyone like him. Most other 'networkers' that I have met will make a lot of promises but don't live up to their words.

Charles Ruffolo is truly The NetworKing."

- Robert Ruijssenaars, Country Manager
Ernest & Julio Gallo Winery, The Netherlands

AFTERWORD

10 YEARS AND COUNTING:

Successes stories and new developments

In the 10 years since I began The Network Club concept – now with thousands of members – and subsequently The NetworKing B.V., I've turned the art of networking into a science – a global science. Worldwide, over 50,000 business professionals currently connect with us and employ this science in their daily businesses and lives.

A flourishing company, The NetworKing B.V. has seen many successes since this book was first published in 2004. From corporate seminars, personalized training, lectures, publications (including 'Ruffle Shuffle', a NetworKing card game), special events and a wide range of personalized NetworKing services to a brand new 'The NetworKing Academy', The NetworKing concept has grown by leaps and bounds – with no end in sight. Leaders from all walks of life, as witnessed by the following success stories, are realizing the tremendous impact that networking can have. The NetworKing B.V. is there to guide them and help them to connect in ways that they never dreamed possible.

The NetworKing goes global!

Befitting our 10-year anniversary, 'The NetworKing concept' has now, as of 2010, expanded into 10 countries around the world... and counting – providing all global members and clients with greater network possibilities and, therefore, a wealth of business opportunities. Striving to become the best and largest professional network organization in the world, we currently have professional networkers carrying on 'The NetworKing creed' in the following countries:

The Netherlands (currently 10 Country/Chapter Holders in various provinces), Belgium, Spain, Portugal, Turkey, USA, China, Africa, India, Emirate of Dubai, European Union/Commission (EU/EC)

(L to R) Charles Ruffolo (Founder and President, The NetworKing B.V.), Shirley van Maanen (The NetworKing, Netherlands), Evelyn van Maanen (The Network Club, The Hague), Sir Richard Branson (Founder and President, Virgin Group), Lucien Tjon (The NetworKing, China), Nafizte Sener (The NetworKing, Turkey) and Bert Fraiquin (The Network Club, Maastricht, Netherlands)

By connecting the networks of our Country/Chapter Holders in other countries, local networks now have the potential to expand rapidly across borders. Our international network is growing exponentially as a result of these new Country/Chapter Holders. Indeed, the NetworKing spiral is boundless.

With the launch of this new Country/Chapter Holder business plan in 2008, professional networkers have the opportunity to enhance and professionalize their existing network organization, or to start a new organization in their own market/area, based on The NetworKing concept. Country/Chapter Holders are provided with an elaborate and comprehensive platform with both online environments as well as traditional, in-person networking opportunities for business.

Anyone interested in becoming a NetworKing Country/Chapter Holder should contact me directly at:

Ruf@TheNetworKing.com.

The NetworKing Academy opens at Nyenrode Business University

Based on the foundations and principles of The NetworKing concept, together with Gerard van Vliet, I co-founded The NetworKing Academy – the first of its kind in the world – which opened with its first official course in September 2010 at the Netherlands' top business school, Nyenrode Business University in Breukelen – only 20 minutes from Amsterdam's Schiphol airport and center of town. Located in a castle and estate whose foundation dates from 1275, the setting for The NetworKing Academy is incomparable.

Through a tailored program, The NetworKing Academy's goal is to enlighten graduates with corporate and entrepreneurial network-related topics in the spirit of The NetworKing concept, as well as professional leadership skills, in order to prepare them to become highly-trained, professional networkers, in various walks of life – to become 'NetWork Wiser®'.

Target audience is the motivated, experienced, mid-career individual with a desire to improve his or her networking abilities and opportunities. Students typically have a Bachelors degree (or equivalent) and a minimum of one year, post-graduate professional experience, along with a good command of the English language. The program, conducted in Dutch and English, lasts three months (12 sessions, one evening per week), starting with a NetworKing Team Building weekend.

International perspective and diversity are key elements of the program.

For more information of The NetworKing Academy at Nyenrode Business University, see:

www.TheNetworKingAcademy.com or e-mail me directly at: Ruf@TheNetworKing.com.

The Clinton Global Initiative (CGI): 2005 – Present
With the Honorable William Jefferson Clinton, 42nd President of The United States

Charles Ruffolo, Founder and President, The NetworKing B.V., with former US President William Jefferson Clinton and Herma Ruffolo-Broesder

Paul R. Ruffolo, J.D., Founder Ruffolo Associates LLP (United States), with former US President Clinton

Over the past few years, I have arranged and hosted to The Netherlands by former US President Clinton – visits that have culminated in several foundations and joint business initiatives between us.

One of the most important and rewarding outcomes of these visits has been my involvement in The Clinton Global Initiative (CGI) – whereby we have developed many partnerships with companies throughout Europe. The CGI was launched in 2005 as part of The William J. Clinton Foundation, established by the former President himself, with the stated mission to "strengthen the capacity of people throughout the world to meet the challenges of global interdependence". The Foundation focuses on four critical areas: health security; economic empowerment; leadership development and citizen service; and racial, ethnic and religious reconciliation. Working principally through partnerships with like-minded individuals, organizations, corporations, and governments, this Foundation often serves as an incubator for new policies and programs.

As part of that Foundation, the Clinton Global Initiative convenes global leaders to devise and implement innovative solutions to the world's most pressing problems.

One of our most successful and rewarding endeavors was to bring The Clinton Foundation together with the Dutch Postcode Lottery, which agreed to donate 1.5 million Euros per year (for five years) to the former President's Foundation. This is a classic example of networking – of connecting people with needs and solutions. It all started in 2005 when the Dutch PostCode Lottery approached my organization, The NetworKing B.V., and used our services to assess the future success of entering new markets. Our recommendation was a partnership with an international company or spokesperson that would provide international recognition of their product. By connecting the dots with an already-forged relationship with former President Clinton, they were able to negotiate a partnership between The Clinton Foundation and the Dutch PostCode Lottery. And by using the 'Clinton' brand, the PostCode Lottery was able to nationalize their product and initiate the process of launching a PostCode Lottery in other countries.

As an added benefit of this 'networking in action', many companies and private individuals have now had the pleasure of not only meeting the former President but also doing business with him.

Bringing parties together during the Clinton Global Initiative (CGI), NYC

Bringing parties together during the Clinton Global Initiative (CGI), NYC

Finalizing the partnership at former US President Clinton's home

Former US Predisent Clinton promoting the Dutch PostCode Lottery

Emergya Wind Technologies

Bringing parties together during the Clinton Global Initiative (CGI), New York City 2007

Emergya Wind Technologies' CEO Gerry van der Sluys (L), discussing wind farm infrastructure with the Governor of Montana, Governor Brian Schweitzer (R)

One of the major partnerships that came out of my involvement with the Clinton Global Initiative was that which we successfully negotiated between CGI and the Dutch wind energy company, Emergya Wind Technologies (EWT). In 2007, EWT agreed to become a primary sponsor of the Annual Meeting of the Clinton Global Initiative in New York City – a sponsorship that would potentially lead to a working relationship between the two entities, with potential sales for EWT and public relations opportunities for both.

How did all this evolve? By networking, of course. Through CGI's important mission and venue we were able to facilitate a presentation by Emergya Wind Technologies and also to introduce the principle members of the company to various Heads of State and other influential individuals. Valuable connections were made and, by sitting down face to face with the ultimate decision-makers – United States Governors as well as large corporations and investors – EWT was able to accomplish more in four days than they had in a full year of operation. That's the power of networking.

The beauty of networking, however, is that it never stops. Our involvement with these two parties led to another very important connection. The NetworKing B.V. succeeded in bringing EWT together with General Wesley K. Clark (retired General of the United States Army, former Commander of NATO, and presidential candidate for the American elections in 2002), a connection that culminated in a contract for General Clark to act as a member of EWT's Board of Directors as well as the acting Director of EWT Americas. Further, my organization was strategically involved in the market and business development of EWT in the expansion of their business in the United States.

Initial 'Meet & Greet' at the Clinton Global Initiative (CGI), New York City 2007

Finalizing the negotiations in Amsterdam, and subsequent signing of the contract

RIG Investments

Connections between energy and former President Clinton led to another major business opportunity that I was able to initiate and facilitate. In 2007 – the same year as the EWT networking connection – I was contacted by RIG Investments N.V. to help expand their investment opportunities in the renewable energy sector. RIG Investments is a venture capitalist, located in Amsterdam. By utilizing my working relationship with the Clinton Global Initiative, we were successful in providing RIG with various investment channels, simply by sitting down with individuals like Carlos Slim (Mexican businessman, philanthropist, Chairman and CEO of Telmex, Telcel and América Móvil and, as of April 2010, cited as 'the wealthiest person in the world', with a net worth of around US$60.6 billion), and Dr. Sultan Al Jaber, CEO of Masdar (a global leader in the push for new low carbon energy technologies and clean, sustainable ways of living), as well as a private meeting with former President Clinton and Henk J. Keilman, President of RIG Investments.

Former US President Clinton with Henk J. Keilman, Founder & CEO, RIG Investments

Henk J. Keilman (L), Founder & CEO of RIG Investments, with Carlos Slim (R), President and CEO of Telmex, Telcel and América Móvil – cited as 'the wealthiest person in the world' (2010)

Dr. Sultan Al Jaber (L), CEO of the Masdar Initiative, with Charles Ruffolo (M), Founder and President, The NetworKing B.V., and Henk J. Keilman (R), Founder & CEO, RIG Investments

Big Improvement Day

In line with this energy thread, in 2007 and 2008, The NetworKing B.V. was successful in marketing and promoting a new initiative in the Netherlands called 'Big Improvement Day' (BID), now an annual event that focuses on the various forms of business development for renewable energy options available in our world today. BID is organized by Winkelman en Van Hessen, a leading communications consultancy that excels in strategic and creative advice, in brand PR, corporate communications, public affairs, crisis communications and special events. With a primary focus on their Dutch homeland, BID's founders invite philanthropists, inventors and corporations from around the globe to attend their event – an event where good ideas are given a chance, partnerships are forged, and networking takes place at a very high level.

Part of presenting this high-level networking was to attain a high-profile, keynote speaker for a fast-paced networking event that we organized for BID – an event that would showcase their renewable energy platform. Who better than Sir Richard Branson (best known for his Virgin brand of over 360 companies) to attract an audience? I'm pleased to say that we were successful in booking and personally escorting Sir Richard Branson to the Big Improvement Day, thereby increasing BID's ticket sales and drawing attention to their important mission.

Big Improvement Day (BID), with guest of honor Sir Richard Branson, Founder and President, Virgin Group (Center top photo): (L to R) Tjarda Voorneman, Special Event Manager, Winkelman en Van Hessen, Sir Richard Branson, Founder and President, Virgin Group, Hanneke Verburg, Director, Winkelman en Van Hessen and Ralph van Hessen, Partner, Winkelman en Van Hessen

Sir Richard Branson, Founder and President, Virgin Group

Exact Software

Following in the same vein, The NetworKing B.V. was approached by Exact Software, a leading developer of business software solutions (including ERP, HRM, CRM, CPM, project management and electronic workflow) to provide a high level of media exposure and brand enhancement for their company. Headquartered in the Netherlands, Exact Software has a global network with offices in more than 40 countries. Using a worldwide sales-driven campaign, we combined a networking session with Sir Richard Branson to reinforce the common set of values that Exact Software has built into their global corporation, specifically their business culture and principles of management and leadership. By connecting our network with *their* corporate values (honesty, trust, respect, integrity, commitment, courage, fun and passion), The NetworKing B.V. assisted Exact Software in reaching their goal of a higher level of media exposure and brand awareness for their broad international platform.

Based on our The NetworKing plan, we emphasized that one's entrepreneurial spirit will leverage effective networking at all times. Exact Software took on that precept, and we now provide networking training for Exact Software employees globally, and have partnered with the corporation on several business-driven projects.

Rajesh Patel, CEO Exact Holding N.V., with Charles Ruffolo, Founder and President, The NetworKing B.V.

Personnel from Exact Software with Sir Richard Branson, Founder and President, Virgin Group

Stedman Graham & Associates: Leaders in Diversity

Stedman Graham – well-known as the life partner of Oprah Winfrey – wanted to take his own brand and corporate identity international, as entrepreneur and CEO of S. Graham & Associates, a Chicago-based corporate and educational marketing and consulting firm. In response, in 2007 and 2008 we helped to create, promote and market the event 'Diversity: Leaders Not Labels' featuring Mr. Graham. By utilizing The NetworKing B.V., Stedmam Graham & Associates has now created an international brand awareness of his company and products as a bona fide business with sustainability. As a direct result of our actions, he has realized an increase in profits, especially in the international market.

Stedman Graham, Founder Stedman Graham & Associates, with Charles Ruffolo, Founder and President, The NetworKing B.V.

Professor Steven R. Schuit, Chairman of the Giving Back Foundation and Legal Counsel for Allen & Overy

In addition, we've worked hand-in-hand with Mr. Graham and DutchVersity/Hi5. Dionne Abdoelhafiezkhan, founder of DutchVersity/Hi5, a cross-media knowledge and network organization with a different sound, built a unique partnership with Mr. Graham. Hi5 is the methodology of DutchVersity. There are several ways to realize your dreams, but in all cases you will have to take action by yourself. Hi5 makes your hands a compass that guides you towards your goal: Passion, Focus, Overview, Reliability and Knowledge.

And last but not least, we've successfully established the Stedman Graham Nyenrode Giving Back Scholarship for a deserving student from the Giving Back Foundation in The Netherlands.

Special connections to special individuals

Using the power of The NetworKing network, clients and members can request tailor-made network solutions with The NetworKing Personal Network Service. With access to decision-makers, financial institutions, venture capitalists, international networks, VIPs and government officials, The

NetworKing Personalized Network Service offers the ideal tool for professionals looking for that hard-to-reach goal, target or contact.

Here is a sampling of our successful connections:

John A. Fentener van Vlissingen (L), Founder and Chairman, BCD Holdings N.V., with General Wesley K. Clark (R), retired General of the United States Army & former Commander of NATO

Former US President Clinton with Dionne Abdoelhafiezkhan, Founder, DutchVersity/Hi5

Henk J. Keilman with Hillary Clinton, Secretary of State

Update: Giving Back Foundation

Established in 1999, the Giving Back Foundation, an outcrop of The NetworKing B.V., continues to grow immensely. As discussed in the Appendix of this book, this Foundation is a non-profit organization committed to bringing critical resources to the youth that need them. Its goal is to energize professional organizations, businesses and high schools to encourage ethnic immigrant youth that are high achievers and motivated but need encouragement from adult role models.

Since 1999, the Giving Back Foundation has helped young people from all over the world. These individuals have learned through their experience with Giving Back that they are able to meet and work with people from extremely diverse backgrounds – especially those in our 'target countries' of India, Taiwan, Egypt and Pakistan. While these young people are brought up in very diverse home environments, our goal is not to change them, but to help and guide them.

To date, the Giving Back Foundation is operating in more than 24 high schools in all the major cities in the Netherlands. Hundreds of youth from 15 countries have gone through our Giving Back program, thanks to our many sponsors and mentors from all walks of the business community.

Giving Back is essentially 'networking to help others'. We give back the same benefits that we reap.

Former US President Clinton with Charles Ruffolo, Founder and President, The NetworKing B.V. and Giving Back Foundation members

Sir Richard Branson, Founder and President, Virgin Group and Charles Ruffolo, Founder and President, The NetworKing B.V., with members of the Giving Back Foundation Student Community

The Giving Back Student Community (2010)

Students who have properly completed the Giving Back program and study at universities or colleges may become members of the Giving Back Student Community, a club that is run by students.

The GBSC organizes many activities, study tours and (sporting) events, designed for the students during their studies, to complete all the knowledge and skills and to give insights which they need to build a successful career in business or government after graduation. The GBSC finances these activities through membership fees, a contribution from students and financial support from the Giving Back Foundation.

Membership in the GBSC also offers students the opportunity to be coached by a professional during their studies. This coach is employed by one of the partners/main sponsors of Giving Back.

More information can be found at www.giving.back.nl.

APPENDIX

GIVING BACK FOUNDATION

(Stichting Giving Back, The Netherlands)

Founded in 1999 by Charles D. A. Ruffolo, MPA

You make a living by what you get,
You make a life by what you give – Sir Winston Churchill

"Giving Back" is a non-profit Foundation committed toward bringing critical resources to the youth that need them. The Giving Back Foundation helps high- school students whose career perspectives, due to their backgrounds, are not on the same level as their talent and ambition. Giving Back offers, to mostly immigrant youth, a group and mentor program to help them broaden their knowledge and experience. Giving Back only functions from private donations from companies and people who want to give back to society. Giving Back does not receive government funding.

MISSION

The mission of the Giving Back (GB) Foundation is to provide access to the fundamental tools and needs in order for ethnic minority (immigrant) youth between the ages of 15 to 18 years in the Netherlands to have opportunities that they would not have normally received, to lead happier, healthier and more productive lives.

GOALS

The goal of the Giving Back Foundation is to help immigrant youth to successfully complete their high school education and enter post-secondary education, internships, apprenticeships, vocational training or the business world. This is according to the life plans and personal goals set by the students during personal development sessions of the Giving Back program.

Giving Back's secondary goal is to assist the students in self-development towards becoming conscientious, independent, informed and responsible adults.

TASK

The task of the Giving Back Foundation is to energize professional organizations, the business communities and high schools to encourage ethnic minority youth that are high achievers and motivated but need encouragement from role models. Through the use of a balanced mentoring program for two years, a high school student operates year-round with a business consultant to improve his or her academic performance, to set career goals, to learn job skills and to develop high work standards in order to grow up as a productive citizen.

OBJECTIVES

The objectives of the Giving Back Foundation are to get individuals and organizations to pledge their time, treasures and resources toward helping the youth; to provide access to the eight phases of the program; to provide the youth with comprehensive training, hands-on business involvement and powerful life-changing experiences which will develop their leadership skills, self-esteem, help them refine career goals and prepare them to lead the search for solutions to the social problems facing them.

GIVING BACK VALUES

- HOPE
- ENTHUSIASM
- RESPECT
- RESPONSIBILITY
- GENEROSITY

BACKGROUND

Immigrants have entered the Netherlands in increasing numbers during the last three decades. They now constitute about 17% of the population. Because many immigrants started at the lowest economic levels, immigrant families are overly represented in the below-average income categories.

Immigrant youth are talented and often motivated but lack good role models, expertise, know-how and personal confidence to successfully enter the business world. They are (and feel they are) at a disadvantage when compared to the majority of traditional Dutch youth.

The Giving Back Foundation was started in 1999 by me, Professional Networker Charles Ruffolo and twelve students from the Haarlem Business School. The objective is to increase the self-motivation and self-confidence of the targeted youth.

METHODOLOGY

Giving Back selects the (potentially) most talented first and second-generation immigrant youth in schools with a high proportion of immigrants. Typically, the students are from 15 to 18 years old, and have two full (secondary) school years remaining.

Each student is assigned a mentor from the business community that is outside the family circle. The mentor is a "career coach", helping the student to expand his or her thinking about the career opportunities that exist and how to reach them.

During the first year, Giving Back students attend monthly workshops, social outings, and business visitations – all designed to increase their self-esteem and self-confidence. During the second year, students assist with the next group as teen consultants and role models.

Giving Back gets support from the business community that opens its doors to immigrants and increases it accessibility for them. The business community contributes mentors, financing, programs, and facilities to demonstrate its high level of interest in giving immigrant youth an equal chance.

WORKING METHOD

To establish its goals, Giving Back has developed a mentor program and an educational program with eight phases that are supported by Key Players.

The Key Players are all linked together to support the Giving Back total community approach: the students, parents, schools, mentors and sponsors or friends. Below is a description of these Key Players:

Key Players

* Students

Students identified by their teachers have a lot of potential for advancement, but are restricted or limited because of their situation.

Students contact their school's counselor for an application. The student must have parental permission to enroll in the Program.

The student will spend monthly one-on-one time with a mentor who will coach and mentor the student. The participating student will be asked to attend orientation sessions and workshops held at different locations. With the mentor, the student will attend social outings that allow him or her to experience first-hand the social climate of business. The student and mentor will participate in a group team-building and motivation training held during the one weekend where students and mentors participate together in outdoor activities to bond with each other. Both will be involved in a community service project where student and mentor support a neighborhood project to "give back" through community service.

Participating students will follow the eight-phase program for two years. If the students are willing to commit the time and effort to building their future, there is a mentor waiting to work with them.

* Parents

The parents stand behind their children and support them as they make their way through their daily lives.

The parents of Giving Back students must first give consent for their child to participate in the Program. If the parents' son/daughter is accepted in the Program, the parents must be committed toward supporting the Program in any positive way they can.

The parents must also give their permission for their son's/daughter's academic records to be shared with the mentor in the Program as needed. The mentors are available to work with the parents to assist in developing their son/daughter to be the best that he/she can be. Therefore, the parents' commitment toward supporting the Program is just as important to themselves as it is to the student.

* High Schools

The high schools are selected based on their location and demographics. The counselors promote and screen possible candidates from their schools.

The counselor will submit a student application and profile for each student selected for participation into the Program. The school counselor may provide the mentor with the student's academic records. This includes the student's high school transcript, report cards and progress reports.

* Mentors

The mentors are usually employees of business, such as entrepreneurs, managers, administrators, technicians, and secretaries, as well as teachers. They all share the common desire to help students prepare for the world of work after graduation. Some are recent graduates themselves, or parents of teens. Others are just concerned about giving someone the personal and career direction they themselves never had.

The mentor will also spend one-on-one time with a student in the Program. The mentors are offering the students their friendship. This one-on-one time will give the student and the mentor an opportunity to get to know each other better and learn from each other. The mentor will also assist the student in becoming the best that he or she can be academically. Additionally, the mentors will attend, with the students, workshops, social outings, a weekend team-building session, and community service work.

One of the primary responsibilities of the mentor is to work with the student to identify occupational interests and develop a plan of action for getting a job, post-secondary education, or if the student chooses, a military career.

The mentor has a role as an intermediary between the business community and the social environment of the student and the school of the student. The mentor is the one who can give direct answers on all the questions a student might have concerning his or her future career. The mentor will coach the assigned student for two years.

The mentors put their unique skills, talents, abilities and resources towards improving the lives of the youth.

* Friends/Sponsors

Sponsors and companies support Giving Back with either monetary or non-monetary contributions. These organizations incorporate the full array of their services, products, human resource policies, business plans, marketing and public relations and overall business philosophy to assist the students.

MEASUREMENT OF SUCCESS FOR GIVING BACK STUDENTS

Giving Back measurements of success are derived directly from the Program's mission and goal. Giving Back is designed to equip young people with the basic tools and resources that create opportunities for success.

The success of Giving Back's program can be measured by the attainment rate of the individual goals in the following categories: secondary education, further education/training, social skills, citizenship, communication, IT, human rights, community service and extracurricular activities (e.g. sports, music, dance, work).

Giving Back has set the following measurements of success by:

1. *Having students create a career path.*
   How? By having mentors work together with students to identify occupational interests and develop a plan of action for getting a job or post-secondary education.

   How? By inspiring students to take charge of their own situations information and knowledge in a new and interesting fashion.

2. *Inspiring the students to pull themselves out of their social and economic situation.*
   How? By increasing the student's knowledge about the employment market and career opportunities.

   How? By learning skills and gaining social experiences that will encourage students to work and contribute to society and their community.

3. *Providing the students with a new sense of direction and self-esteem.*
   How? By establishing positive relationships and role models that can last throughout the students' lives.

   How? By providing a sense of personal reward for the mentors by helping students excel academically and personally.

The success of Giving Back will extend far beyond its own lifetime. It will be a lasting legacy, enriching the lives of future generations.

If you would like to either volunteer as a mentor or contribute your time or financial support for the Giving Back Foundation, please contact us in the Netherlands as follows:

+(31) (0)20 623 41 71
Stichting Giving Back
Frederiksplein 1-4hg
1017 XK Amsterdam
The Netherlands
E-mail: info@givingback.nl
www.givingback.nl

Ruffolo has been nominated (2003) for "Hero of the Year" by KRO broadcasting in The Netherlands.

Beginning in January of 2004, a partner branch of the Giving Back Foundation will be launched in Singapore, under the direction of Erik van Vulpen.

www.Giving-Back.com

Ruffolo's Professional Memberships and Affiliations

President – Amsterdam American Business Club (AABC)

Membership Committee Member – American Chamber of Commerce in

The Netherlands (AmCham)

Board member – Connect International Business Club, The Netherlands

Board member – C3 Company-Club-Challenger, The Netherlands

Board member – Multicultural Network Rijksambtenaren

Advisory Board – NFL European League

Committee Member – Holland America Foundation (H.A.F.)

Sponsor – The John Adams Institute, The Netherlands

Sponsor – ACCESS, The Netherlands

Sponsor – Nationaal Fonds Kinderhulp (NFK), The Netherlands

Sponsor – Glenn Mills School, Wezep, The Netherlandss

Member – Den Haag (The Hague) International Business Club

Member – Rotterdam American Business Club, The Netherlands

Member – The Koperen Hoogte Business Club, The Netherlands

Member – Amstel Business Club, The Netherlands

Member – Meppel Business Club, The Netherlands

Founder – Giving Back Foundation, The Netherlands (www.GivingBack.nl)

Co-Founder – The NetworKing Academy (www.TheNetworKingAcademy.com)

Advisory Board/Partner – Big Improvement Day (BID)

Contact information

Charles D. A. Ruffolo, MPA,

Professional Networker, Speaker, Author, Publisher & Trainer

Founder/owner:

The NetworKing BV & RIBS Network

www.TheNetworKing.com

The Network Club

www.TheNetworkClub.com

The NetworKing Academy

www.TheNetworKingAcademy.com

E-mail: Ruf@TheNetworKing.com

Telephone: +31 (0)521 510 139

Mobile: +31 (0)6 502 876 72

Fax: +31 (0)521 510 179

Kallenkote 31a

8345 HC Kallenkote

The Netherlands

A very special thanks to Vanessa Siegal, Managing Director of SpiralFX Interactive, LLC, until 2008, a Web and Internet application development and design company, responsible for the development, enhancement and design of all the RIBS Network, The Network Club and Giving Back Foundation Web sites.

www.spiralfx.com

Special attention to Willem & Nella Pit for their remarkable commitment to The NetworKing concept – Thank you!